THE
RIGHTS OF
THE POOR

THE AMERICAN CIVIL LIBERTIES UNION HANDBOOK SERIES

AN AMERICAN
CIVIL LIBERTIES
UNION HANDBOOK

THE
RIGHTS OF
THE POOR

Sylvia Law
with a chapter on
The Rights of Migrants
by BURT NEUBORNE

General Editors of this series:
Norman Dorsen, *General Counsel*
Aryeh Neier, *Executive Director*
Special Editor:
Ruth Bader Ginsburg, *Coordinator,*
  ACLU Women's Rights Project

A Richard Baron Book
Sunrise Books, Inc. / E. P. Dutton & Co., Inc.

Published simultaneously in Canada by Clarke, Irwin & Company
Limited, Toronto and Vancouver

ISBN: 0-87690-139-9
Library of Congress Catalog Number: 74-75008

Table of Contents

THE
RIGHTS OF
THE POOR

Preface

This guide sets forth your rights under present law and offers suggestions on how you can protect your rights. It is one of a series of guidebooks published in cooperation with the American Civil Liberties Union on the rights of teachers, servicemen, mental patients, prisoners, students, criminal suspects, women, and the very poor.

The hope surrounding these publications is that Americans informed of their rights will be encouraged to exercise them. Through their exercise, rights are given life. If they are rarely used, they may be forgotten and violations may become routine.

This guide offers no assurances that your rights will be respected. The laws may change and, in some of the subjects covered in these pages, they change quite rapidly. An effort has been made to note those parts of the law where movement is taking place but it is not always possible to predict accurately when the law *will* change.

Even if the laws remain the same, interpretations of them by courts and administrative officials often vary. In a federal system such as ours, there is a built-in problem of the differences between state and federal law, not to speak of the confusion of the differences from state to state. In addition, there are wide variations in the ways in which particular courts and administrative officials will interpret the same law at any given moment.

If you encounter what you consider to be a specific abuse of your rights you should seek legal assistance. There are a number of agencies that may help you, among them ACLU affiliate offices, but bear in mind that the ACLU is a limited-purpose organization. In many communities, there are federally funded legal service offices which provide assistance to poor persons who cannot afford the costs of legal representation. In general, the rights that the ACLU defends are freedom of inquiry and expression; due process of law; equal protection of the laws; and privacy. The authors in this series have discussed other rights in these books (even though they sometimes fall outside the ACLU's usual concern) in order to provide as much guidance as possible.

These books have been planned as guides for the people directly affected: therefore the question and answer format. In some of these areas there are more detailed works available for "experts." These guides seek to raise the largest issues and inform the non-specialist of the basic law on the subject. The authors of the books are themselves specialists who understand the need for information at "street level."

No attorney can be an expert in every part of the law. If you encounter a specific legal problem in an area discussed in one of these guidebooks, show the book to your attorney. Of course, he will not be able to rely *exclusively* on the guidebook to provide you with adequate representation. But if he hasn't had a great deal of experience in the specific area, the guidebook can provide some helpful suggestions on how to proceed.

Norman Dorsen, General Counsel
American Civil Liberties Union

Aryeh Neier, Executive Director
American Civil Liberties Union

Introduction

This book was written for the poor, and for those working with them. I have tried to keep the language simple, without being simple-minded. This is always a difficult job, especially for someone with the benefit of legal training.

A poor person needs concrete information to obtain the subsistence benefits to hold life together. He or she often also needs help in dealing with the system. The information which this book provides is often not very concrete, because conditions and rules vary so much from place to place, and the rules change from day to day. Help from a friend, a welfare-rights worker, a community organizer, or lawyer must be found at the local level. At best this book is just a starting place for a poor person struggling to get the things which the law guarantees.

Richard Nixon's second term of office has brought important restrictions in the rights of the poor. While Watergate captures national attention and headlines, the Department of Health, Education and Welfare quietly abolishes rights and protections which have been afforded the poor by federal regulation since the New Deal. Repression and cutbacks at the state and local levels are perhaps even more serious.

There is a disturbing irony in the commercial publication and sale of a book for the poor. If this is to be of

any use to the people for whom it is intended, it will
be because more affluent people and organizations buy
copies and make them available without charge to poor
people.

Many people deserve thanks. First, the welfare recipients, organizers, and lawyers who put themselves on the
line and poured enormous dedication and energy into the
struggles which make it possible to talk about rights for
poor people. Second, many people provided so much direct
help that I feel that I did little more than orchestrate
their work. For this generosity, I am enormously grateful
to: Laura Allto, Adele Blong, Henry Freedman, Andrea
Malak, Melsenior McDaniel, William Phillips, Ronald
Pollack, Nancy Duff Levy, Louise Lander, Barbara Rios,
and Linda Rollyson.

Who are the poor in America?

Most Americans are poor at one time or another during their lives. Many Americans are poor all of their lives.
The United States Department of Labor estimated that in
1970 an urban family of four needs $10,664 to live at a
moderate level. At the same time the mean income of
white men in America was $10,634. The mean income
of black men was $6,773, of white women it was $5,965,
and of black women it was $4,943. Thus most American
families are officially poor. If you are a woman, or old,
or black, the likelihood of being poor is even greater. Poor
people are the real majority.

What special rights do poor people have?

Poor people have the right to receive welfare, free
medical care, food stamps, and free or low-cost school
lunches. These rights are discussed in this book. In addition, poor people have rights to: public housing, free

legal services; go to court without paying court fees in some cases; day care and other social services; unemployment compensation; tuition reductions or scholarships; school breakfasts; and special food programs for the elderly. These rights are not discussed in this book because there is not enough space to talk about all of the rights of all of the poor.

Are these legal rights?

Yes. All the rights discussed in this book are legal rights. If the department of welfare fails to give you the benefits to which you are entitled, within the required time limits, they are breaking the law. Welfare, free medical care, food stamps, and free school lunches are not charity. They are the legal rights of people who meet the qualifications for them.

Every American has the right to fair treatment from the government. You have the right to apply for any benefit, to be informed of the law and be treated in accordance with the written rules and regulations governing the administration of benefits, and to appeal any unfavorable decision made by the administrators.

How can people get their rights?

There are several organizations throughout the country that help poor people get their rights. The most important of these are organizations made up of poor people themselves. These welfare rights and tenant organizations provide information, help people apply for aid, refer them to lawyers, and put people with similar problems in touch with one another.

If you need help in finding a poor people's organization in your area, or in starting a new organization, get in contact with:

National Welfare Rights Organization
1424 16th Street
Washington, D.C. 20036
(202) 483-1531

National Tenants Organization
425 Thirteenth Street, N.W.
Washington, D.C. 20004
(202) 347-3358

To find lawyers specializing in poverty law you should look in the telephone book under Community Legal Services, Neighborhood Legal Services, American Civil Liberties Union, Urban Coalition, or National Lawyers Guild. If you have trouble finding a good local lawyer or if you believe that your lawyer is not doing a good job, one of the following people or organizations may be able to help you:

Welfare: Henry Freedman, Esq.
Columbia Center on Social Welfare Law
25 West 43rd Street
New York, N.Y. 10036
(212) 354-7670

Housing: National Housing Law Project
Earl Warren Legal Institute
University of California
Berkeley, Calif. 94720
(415) 642-2826

Health: National Health and Environmental Law Project
UCLA Law School, 405 Hilgard Avenue
Los Angeles, Calif. 90024
(213) 825-7601

Food: Ron Pollack, Esq.
Food Research and Action Center
25 West 43rd Street
New York, N.Y. 10036
(212) 354-7670

I
Welfare

GENERAL

What is welfare?
Welfare is money paid by the state or federal government to people who don't have enough to provide for their essential needs—food, rent and clothing. Need is the basic requirement for receiving welfare.

Who can get welfare?
Anybody can apply for welfare. You won't necessarily get what you ask for, but you must be allowed to fill out an application, be told the reasons if your application is denied, be shown the law, and be given a right to appeal if your request for aid is denied.[1]

During the Depression the federal government began welfare programs. Four especially needy categories of Americans are entitled to federally financed welfare: the aged, the blind, the permanently and totally disabled, and families with dependent children. The federal government

---

[1] 45 C.F.R. §206.10(a) (4).

makes money available to the states to provide welfare
to people in these categories. The states provide matching
funds and run the welfare program. In order to receive
federal money for welfare for people in these categories,
the states must run a program that meets federal requirements. These categorical welfare programs are discussed in Chapters I and II.

People who do not fall into one of these categories may
be eligible for general assistance. Most states provide some
general assistance to some people who are poor but who
are not aged, blind, disabled or a member of a family
with dependent children. Every state makes its own rules
for general assistance. There are no federal requirements.
The amounts that the states pay for general assistance
are generally less than the amounts paid to poor people
in the federal categories. General assistance is discussed in
Chapter III.

Where do you get welfare?

There is a welfare office in every county and in all but
the smallest towns. You must apply for welfare at your
local office. The welfare department must have some offices open twenty-four hours a day, seven days a week, to
provide help in obtaining emergency medical care and
services.[2]

How do you apply for welfare?

You apply in person at your local welfare office. You
must sign an official application form. If you need help,
you can bring a friend or a welfare-rights worker with
you when you apply and that person can stay with you
and represent you throughout the whole application pro-

---

[2] 45 C.F.R. §206.10(a) (5).

cess.[3] If you are incapacitated or incompetent, a friend
or relative must be allowed to apply for you.[4]

When you apply for welfare you should take with you,
or send to the department, any papers you have that
show how much money you need (e.g., rent receipts); the
composition of your family and the ages of the children
(e.g., birth certificates); and your income (e.g., pay stubs).
It will be easier if you can take or send as much of this
kind of information as possible, but if you have trouble
getting the necessary papers together, the welfare department must help you.

How long does it take to get welfare?

The welfare department must make its decision and
send you your first check or a notice of the reasons why
aid is being denied within forty-five days after the date
of application.[5] The only cases in which they are allowed
to take longer than forty-five days to decide are:

(1.) When you delay in providing requested information.

(2.) When your application is for aid to the permanently
and totally disabled (where sixty days are allowed).

(3.) When there is some emergency that could not be
prevented or controlled by the welfare department.

If you are found eligible for assistance in some states
you will receive money figured from the day you applied.
You must receive money figured from the thirtieth day
after application.[6] (Sixtieth day after application for Aid to
the Disabled.)

How do you know if you are entitled to get welfare?

When you apply for aid, the welfare department should
give you a booklet describing your rights and the rules

---

[3]45 C.F.R. §206.10(a) (1) (iii).
[4]45 C.F.R. §206.10(a) (1) (ii).
[5]45 C.F.R. §206.10(a) (3).
[6]45 C.F.R. §206.10(a) (6).

written in language that you can understand.[7] If the department denies your application for aid, they must send you a written notice telling you the specific reason that your request for aid was denied. This notice must also tell you that you have the right to request a hearing at which you can challenge the decision, and the procedure for getting such a hearing.[8]

SPECIAL CATEGORIES

Need is the basic requirement for all welfare aid. Need requirements are discussed on p. 34.

Who is eligible for aid to the aged?

Old Age Assistance (OAA) is available to everyone who is: (1) sixty-five years old and over; and (2) not in a public institution such as a prison or a hospital. These are the only requirements. You can get OAA whether or not you have ever had a job or if you have worked as a farmer or domestic laborer. You can get OAA even if you also get Social Security.[9]

Almost everyone over sixty-five is entitled to receive free medical treatment (Medicare) no matter how much money they have. Rights under Medicare are described on pages 92–101 of this book.

Who is eligible for aid to the blind?

You do not have to be totally blind in order to receive Aid to the Blind (AB). You may be eligible for benefits in this category even if you have *partial* sight, but you will

---

[7] 45 C.F.R. §206.10(a) (2).
[8] 45 C.F.R. §206.10(a) (4).
[9] 42 U.S.C. §§301 *et seq.*

be required to take an eye test to prove that your eyesight is extremely poor.[10]

Who is eligible for aid to the permanently and totally disabled?

People who have a physical or mental condition that makes it impossible for them to work are eligible for Aid to the Permanently and Totally Disabled (APTD). The general rule is that you must be able to prove that your condition cannot be cured or improved.[11] If your condition makes you unable to work, APTD cannot be denied just because you are able to take care of yourself at home.[12] The state may not deny APTD just because your disability results from an emotional illness.[18] In practice some states deny APTD to people who are seriously injured while other states give it to almost anyone who has a serious emotional problem or a problem with drinking or drugs. If you cannot work but are denied APTD, you should see a lawyer. No one who is under eighteen or in a public institution is eligible for APTD.

What is Supplemental Security Income?

Beginning Jan. 1, 1974, the present state/federal welfare programs for the aged, the blind, and the disabled will be eliminated. Instead there will be one new Supplemental Security Income program (SSI).[14] SSI will be administered by the federal Social Security Administration. It will be available to United States citizens or aliens admitted for

---

[10]42 U.S.C. §1201 *et seq.*, repealed effective Jan. 1, 1974.

[11]45 C.F.R. §233.80(a) (1), repealed effective Jan. 1, 1974.

[19]*Center v. Vowell*, F.Supp. (W.D.Tex. 1973) 2 CCH Pov. L. Rpt. ¶17, 225, *Dotter v. Martin*, F.Supp. (N.D. Calif. 1973) 2 CCH Pov. L. Rpt. ¶17, 108.

[18]*Fisher v. Graves*, 361 F. Supp. 1356 (S.D. Me. 1973).

[14]Social Security Act, Title XVI, as amended by Public Law 92-603 1972. 42 USCA sec.

permanent residence who are over sixty-five, blind, or disabled. Payments will also be made for "essential persons," such as husbands or wives of eligible aged recipients who have not themselves reached age 65. An "essential person" is defined as a person who for the month of December, 1973 was a person who was not eligible in his or her own right for aid under a state program in effect for June 1973, but who was living with a person who was eligible for welfare and whose needs were taken into account. These provisions for "essential persons" do not apply to people who become eligible for SSI after December 1973.[15]

The basic annual standards for SSI eligibility and payment are as follows:[16]

	Monthly Income	*Resources*
Individual alone	$130	$1500
Two eligible individuals, or eligible individual and an essential person	$195	$2250 $2250

In addition the states are required to provide a supplement to the federal SSI payment to assure that everyone who is receiving AB, APTD, or OAA in December 1973 continues to receive at least as much as they were getting at that time.[17] SSI recipients will not be eligible for food stamps.

In determining the amount of resources available to an SSI applicant, the federal government will disregard a home, household goods, a car, personal effects, and other resources which a blind or disabled person needs as part of a plan for self-support. In determining the amount of

---

[15]Public Law 93-66, approved July 9, 1973.

[16]Effective July 1, 1974 the federal benefits under the SSI program will be increased from $130 to $140 for an individual and from $195 to $210 for a couple.

[17]Public Law 93-66, §212.

income available, the government must disregard the first $240 a year, plus the next $780 a year in earned income, plus half of the rest of the earned income. If a blind or disabled person has a plan for self-support, all income may be disregarded in determining need. Other additional income disregards include: one-third child-support payments, irregular unearned income up to sixty dollars a year, educational scholarships, foster-care payments, home produce consumed at home, and state or local supplemental benefits.[18]

The new program has an "assumed income" rule. This means that it will be assumed that all of the income of an ineligible spouse living in the home is available to the applicant and that parents' income is available to blind or disabled persons under twenty-one living in the parents' home.

Blind and disabled SSI recipients are required to accept state vocational rehabilitation services unless they have good cause to refuse such services. Alcoholics and drug addicts are eligible for SSI benefits only if they are currently undergoing treatment. Payments to such people must be made to another individual who will spend the money for the benefit of the SSI recipient.

Even though the United States Supreme Court has said that residency and citizenship requirements are unconstitutional, the SSI law imposes a thirty-day residency requirement and allows the states to set longer waiting periods for supplemental benefits.

AID TO DEPENDENT CHILDREN

Who is eligible for aid to families with needy dependent children?

To get Aid to Dependent Children (ADC) a family must be needy and have: (1) at least one child; (2) a relative

---

[18]Proposed Regulations, 20 C.F.R. 416.1101 *et seq*. 38 Fed. Reg. 27406, Oct. 3, 1973.

living in the same house as the child; and (3) at least
one parent who cannot or does not support or care for
the child.[19]

Who is a child?

All people under the age of eighteen are children for the
purposes of receiving ADC. Until recently, some states
denied aid to families with children sixteen to eighteen
years old if the child was not in school or was getting
bad grades. Now the Supreme Court says that aid must
be provided to all needy children under eighteen, whether
or not they are in school.[20]

States *may* provide aid to families with children eighteen
to twenty-one years old, if the children regularly attend
school. Some states do not provide aid to families with
children over eighteen.[21] If a state provides ADC to
families with older children in school, it may not refuse
aid because of the *kind* of school the child attends, or
because the child gets bad grades. A poor child may attend
college or vocational or high school and still receive aid.[22]

Federal ADC funds are also available to pregnant
women so they can prepare for the birth of their children
and have an adequate diet during pregnancy. In most
states a woman can apply for ADC or for an increase in
the ADC grant she is already receiving once a doctor has
determined she is pregnant.[23] Some states, however, do

---

[19]42 U.S.C. §606(a).

[20]*Diguesaldo v. Shea,* 404 U.S. 1008 (1972). 45 C.F.R.
§233.90(c) (VI).

[21]Some of these states are Alaska, Delaware, Florida,
Georgia, Mississippi, South Dakota and Wisconsin.

[22]*Townsend v. Swank,* 404 U.S. 282 (1971).

[23]45 C.F.R. §§233.90(c)(2)(ii) and (c)(3). *Alcala v. Burns,*
362 F.Supp. 180, (S.D. Iowa 1973), *Doe v. Lurkard,* 363 F.
Supp. 823 (D.Va. 1973), *Harris v. Mississippi,* 363 F.Supp.
1293 (D.Miss. 1973), *Green v. Stanton,* 364 F.Supp. 123 (D.
Ind. 1973). *Contra, Parks v. Hardin,* 345 F.Supp. 620 (N.D.
Ga. 1973).

not now provide ADC money to pregnant women, although some courts have said that states must do so.[24] If you are pregnant and welfare refuses to give you a full grant for the unborn child, you should see a lawyer.

Who is considered an adult relative of a needy child?

In order to get ADC the relative taking care of the child must be: (1) a relative by blood, marriage, or adoption; and (2) the person who is living with the child.

If a parent is living in the home and taking care of a needy child, the parent should be able to get a grant as a "caretaker relative." Other relatives can also get grants as caretakers if they are living with the child. ADC caretaker relatives may be grandparents, sisters, or brothers, stepparents, stepsisters or brothers, uncles, aunts, cousins, nephews, or nieces who are caring for needy children without parents.[25] Some states, however, do not allow all of these relatives to get grants as caretakers. If you are refused a caretaker grant that you are entitled to under federal law, you should consult a lawyer.[26]

When is a child deprived of the support of one parent?

To be eligible for ADC a child must have at least one parent who is: (1) dead; (2) physically or mentally incapacitated; or (3) away from home.

When is a parent too disabled to support the child?

A child is eligible for ADC, even if both parents are living in the home, if one parent is too physically or

---

[24]*Wilson v. Weaver,* 358 F.Supp. 447 (N.D. Ill., 1972).

[25]42 U.S.C. §606(a) (1).

[26]For example, a federal court struck down a Texas rule that caretaker relatives could not be married, and ordered ADC for a needy family in which the married grandmother was taking care of her grandchildren, *Lopez v. Vowell,* 471 F.2d 690 (5th Cir. 1973), cert. denied, 411 U.S. 939 (1973).

mentally disabled to work. The parent's disability does not need to be permanent or total for the child to receive ADC; it is only necessary that at the present time the parent have "a physical or mental defect, illness, or disability, whatever its cause, degree, or duration, or accompanying factors."[27] If you believe that one parent meets this definition of disability but welfare denies you aid, you should see a lawyer. If you apply for ADC on this basis you will probably be required to have a medical examination.

When is a parent away from home?

This question isn't as easy as it seems. Two examples will illustrate what welfare officials have considered "away from home" to mean.

Mrs. Betty Damico and her husband decided to separate. He left home, and a few days later she applied for welfare. The welfare officials told her that she could not get ADC until she either filed for divorce or waited three months to prove that her husband was really gone. Mrs. Damico consulted a lawyer who brought a lawsuit on her behalf to force the welfare department to give her an ADC grant immediately. The court held that the welfare department cannot require a mother to file for divorce to get ADC;[28] The welfare department cannot set up an arbitrary waiting period before a mother can get ADC to prove that her husband is gone for good.[29] The Nixon administration is now trying to impose waiting requirements, even though the courts say they are illegal.[30]

In several states welfare departments refused to pay

---

[27]45 C.F.R. 233.90(c) (iv).

[28]See also, *Carter v. Stanton*, 405 U.S. 669 (1972), *on remand*, 350 F.Supp. 1337 (S.D. Ind.).

[29]*Damico v. California*, 389 U.S. 416 (1969), *Doe v. Schmidt*, 330 F.Supp. 159 (E.D. Wisc. 1971), *Doe v. Hursh*, 337 F. Supp. 614 (D. Minn. 1970), *Linnane v. Betit*, 331 F.Supp. 868 (D. Vt. 1971).

[30]38 Fed. Reg. 23802 (Sept. 4, 1973).

ADC to mothers of needy children whose fathers were away from home in military service because they said that the fathers were not away permanently. The U.S. Supreme Court has now ruled that a father is absent when he is away doing military service.[81] A father does not need to abandon his children entirely in order for the children to receive ADC. The father can visit the children and the mother occasionally while the family is receiving ADC. The family should not stop receiving aid just because the father occasionally gives the children a small gift or some food. ADC can be stopped only if the father is in the home regularly and only regular contributions for the support of the children are counted in determining the family need.

Can states add other requirements for getting ADC?

No. The basic requirements of ADC eligibility are dependency and need. The Supreme Court has held that the states cannot make up their own additional requirements for receiving ADC.[82] (Work requirements are discussed in Chapter II.)

Many states try to require mothers to do various things to get absent fathers to support needy children. In every state fathers are required to support their children whether or not they are married to the children's mother, and a mother who applies for welfare will be asked to "cooperate" in trying to get support from the absent father before she begins receiving ADC. She does not have to cooperate. The law is now clear that poor families have

---

[81]*Carleson v. Remillard,* 406 U.S. 598 (1972).

[82]*Townsend v. Swank,* 404 U.S. 282 (1971). "At least in the absence of congressional authorization for the exclusion clearly evidenced from the Social Security Act or its legislative history, a state eligibility standard that excludes persons eligible for assistance under federal AFDC standards violates the Social Security Act and is therefore invalid under the Supremacy Clause." 404 U.S. at 286.

a right to get ADC even though the mother refuses to
try to get support from the father.

For example, courts have held that mothers have the
right to continue receiving aid even though they: (1) refuse
to give the name of the father of an illegitimate child;[83]
(2) refuse to file a criminal complaint against the father
for desertion or nonsupport;[84] (3) refuse to file a civil support suit;[85] and (4) refuse to take a lie detector test.[86]
The Nixon administration has recently proposed rules
which would allow welfare to terminate aid in some cases
in which the mother refuses to cooperate in seeking support,[87] but these new rules are probably illegal.[88] If the
welfare department tries to force you to do any of these
things, you should see a lawyer.

Since the courts have made it perfectly clear that aid
may not be reduced or terminated because a mother refuses to cooperate in obtaining support from an absent
father, states have tried to find other ways to force co-

---

[83]*Doe v. Shapiro*, 302 F.Supp. 761 (D. Conn. 1969), *appeal
dismissed*, 396 U.S. 488 (1970), *rehearing denied*, 397 U.S.
970 (1970). *Doe v. Swank*, 332 F.Supp. 61 (N.D. Ill.
1971), Aff'd *sub nom Weaver v. Doe*, 404 U.S. 987 (1971).
Doe v. Harder, 310 F.Supp. 302 (D. Conn. 1970), *appeal dismissed*, 399 U.S. 902 (1970). *Woods v. Miller*, 318 F.Supp. 510
(W.D. Pa. 1971). *Saddler v. Winstead*, 332 F.Supp. 130 (N.D.
Miss. 1971).

[84]*Taylor v. Martin*, 330 F.Supp. 85 (N.D. Calif. 1971),
aff'd *sub nom Carleson v. Taylor*, 404 U.S. 980 (1971). *Shirley
v. Lavine*, 365 F.Supp. 818 (N.D. N.Y. 1973), on remand.

[85]*Doe v. Schmidt*, 330 F.Supp. 159 (E.D. Wis. 1970), *Juras
v. Meyers*, 327 F.Supp. 759 (D. Ore. 1971), aff'd 404 U.S. 803
(1971). *Magness v. Davidson*, —— F.Supp. —— (D. Md.
1972) 2 CCH Pov. L. Rpt. ¶15.051. *Story v. Roberts*, 352 F.
Supp. 473 (W.D. Fla. 1972). *Doe v. Flowers*, 364 F. Supp. 953
(D. W.Va. 1973).

[86]*County of Contra Costa v. Social Welfare Board*, 229 C.A.
2d 762, 40 Cal. Rptr. 605 (1964).

[87]38 Fed. Reg. 10940 (May 3, 1973), amending 45 C.F.R.
§233.90.

[88]*Shirley v. Lavine*, 365 F.Supp. 818, 823 (N.D. N.Y. 1973)
on remand.

operation. One court has held that the state may hold a woman in contempt of court, and send her to jail, if she refuses to name the father of her child receiving ADC.[39]

Can a welfare department cut off a woman's ADC benefits because she has sexual relationships with men?

Not any more, although in the past welfare aid was frequently denied to mothers who had sexual relations or lived with men. The two reasons for this policy were the desire of welfare officials to punish women for their "immoral" conduct, and to make men support the children of the women with whom they had sexual relationships. Various anti-men rules were issued by welfare departments throughout the country. The "man in the house" rule stated that ADC would be denied to a woman if a man visited her home frequently or if she had sexual relations with him. The "substitute father" rule meant that any man who lived in the home with a woman and occasionally acted in a fatherly way to her children would be considered the children's father, whether he was or not, and would therefore be responsible for supporting them. Under the "suitable home" rule aid could be cut off if a woman engaged in any conduct—such as having sexual relations with a man—of which a welfare worker did not approve. These rules frequently resulted in outrageous invasions of welfare recipients privacy by welfare workers who would make surprise visits to a woman to search her house for evidence of a man.

Today all of these rules are illegal. Welfare mothers can have sexual relations or live with a man without losing ADC. There is no reason for a caseworker to ask any questions about a woman's relationships with men. (Of course, a caseworker can ask about any regular source of income.) The Supreme Court has held: (1) the welfare department cannot "discourage immorality and illegitimacy

---

[39]*Doe v. Norton,* 365 F.Supp. 65 (D. Conn. 1973).

by the device of absolute disqualification of needy children"; (2) a "parent" is a person who has a legal obligation to support a child. A mother's boyfriend, or lover, or common law husband, is not the "parent" of children who are not his.[40]

If the welfare department thinks a home is unhealthy or unsafe for children, they can take the mother to court and try to have the children taken away from her by proving that she is neglecting them, that the home environment is harmful to them, and that they would be better cared for someplace else. The welfare department cannot cut off a mother's ADC benefits simply because they think the home is unsuitable for children.[41]

Children cannot be taken away from their mother if the only reason the welfare department thinks the home is unsuitable is because the mother is unmarried. The fact of having borne an illegitimate child or children does not make a woman a bad mother.[42] The welfare department must prove that the mother neglects her children before they can be removed from her care.

Can children continue to get ADC when their mother remarries?

Yes, because although a husband is legally obligated to support his wife, he is not required to support her children by a former husband or other man. Therefore, when a woman who has been receiving ADC marries, her children can still continue to get benefits since they still have only one legal parent—the mother—even though there are now two adults in the home.[48] The Supreme Court has said

[40]*King v. Smith*, 392 U.S. 309 (1968), *affirming on other grounds*, 277 F.Supp. 31 (M.D. Ala. 1967).

[41]45 C.F.R. 233.90(b).

[42]*In Re Cager*, 248 A.2d 384 (Md. 1968); *In Re Nyce*, 268 N.E. 233 (App. Ill. 1971).

[48]The federal rule, which applies everywhere in the United States is "the inclusion in the family, or the presence in the

that children must continue to receive ADC unless the new husband wants to support them and in fact does so on a regular basis.[44] If the stepfather occasionally buys his wife's children food or clothes or a gift, it does not necessarily mean that he has chosen to support them and the welfare department cannot cut off their ADC. Since a stepfather is not required to support his stepchildren, he should not be required to give the welfare department information about his income.[45] Some states have passed special support laws for poor people. These provide that stepfathers are liable for support of their stepchildren if the children would otherwise need welfare. The Supreme Court has declared these special support rules for poor people unconstitutional.[46] Unless *all* stepfathers are required to support their stepchildren, husbands of poor women cannot be forced to do so.[47]

What is aid to an essential person?

Welfare departments sometimes grant additional aid to a family receiving welfare for the support of an "essential person."[48] An essential person is someone who lives in the home of a person receiving categorical aid, is not

---

home, of a 'substitute parent' or 'man-in-the-house' or any individual other than one (legally obligated to support the child under State law of general applicability), is not an acceptable basis for a finding of ineligibility or for assuming the availability of income by the State." 45 C.F.R. §233.90(a).

[44]*Solman v. Shapiro*, 300 F.Supp. 409 (D.C. Conn.), aff'd. 396 U.S. 5 (1969).

[45]*Rosen v. Hursh*, 464 F.2d. 731 (8th Cir. 1972).

[46]Lewis v. Martin (Stark), 312 F.Supp. 197 (N.D. Calif. 1968), 397 U.S. 552 (1970). *Gaither v. Sterrett*, 346 F.Supp. 1095 (N.D. Ind. 1972) aff'd. 409 U.S. 809 (1972). *Bunting v. Juras*, 502 P.2d 607 (Ore. 1972).

[47]In some states, e. g. Iowa, all stepfathers are required to support their stepchildren. *Carrie v. Iowa Dept. of Soc. Service*, 2 CCH Pov. L. Rpt. ¶15,376 (1972).

[48]45 C.F.R. §233.20(b)(3).

personally eligible for assistance, and is "essential to the well-being of the recipient."

For example, if a man over sixty-five is receiving old age assistance, he may also receive aid for the needs of his fifty-eight-year-old wife, if she is "essential to his well-being." Or if a family with a working mother with young children has a sister or a friend living in the house, the family may get money to help meet the needs of this "essential person."

The law concerning essential persons varies from state to state so you should check your own state's particular law if you think you might qualify for aid under it.

Sometimes welfare departments try to use the essential person rule in reverse. That is, they decide that a person living in a welfare household is essential and try to make him support the family if he gets any money. This is illegal. The welfare department cannot force a person to support a family just because he lives with or is important to it. The law obligates only certain persons to support one another. For example, parents must support their children, but brothers and sisters do not have to support each other. This means that if a son over the age of twenty-one lives with his family and stays home to take care of his younger brothers and sisters he may get aid as an essential person. But if he gets a job he cannot be forced to support those children even if he continues to live with them.[49]

----

[49]*Reyna v. Vowell*, 470 F.2d 494 (5th Cir. 1972). *Solman v. Shapiro*, 300 F.Supp. 409, 415, (D. Conn.), aff'd., 396 U.S. 5 (1969), says "the decision as to whether any individual will be recognized as essential to the recipient's well-being shall rest with the recipient . . . The (Department) does not have the right to designate or to assume that a stepfather is an essential person . . ."

AID TO FAMILIES WITH DEPENDENT CHILDREN AND AN UNEMPLOYED FATHER

Can families with two parents in the home ever get ADC?

Yes. In some states ADCU (Aid to Families with Dependent Children and an Unemployed Father) is given to families in which both parents are in the home and the father is unemployed. ADCU is available in fewer than half the states.[50] These states and the amounts paid by them to a family of four are listed in the chart at the back of the book.

When is a father unemployed?

To be considered eligible for ADCU a father must: (1) work less than one hundred hours a month and earn less than enough to meet the family needs;[51] (2) have been unemployed for at least thirty days—more in some states; (3) be willing to accept any *bona fide* offer of work or work training (if he refuses work, ADCU payments may be terminated); and (4) have been employed in the past.

What constitutes a refusal to work?

Before the welfare department can deny or terminate ADCU payments to a family because the father has refused to accept an offer of work, it must: (1) show that there

---

[50]*Henry v. Betit,* 323 F.Supp. 418 (D. Alas. 1971) holds that the Constitution does not require states to have an ADCU program.

[51]45 C.F.R. §233.100. If a father's work is intermittent, he is unemployed if he worked less than one hundred hours a month for the prior two months and is expected to be under the one hundred hours in the next month.

was a definite job offer, at wages which meet minimum wage requirements and which are customary for such work; (2) make sure that the father is physically able to do the work offered; (3) make sure that the father has a reasonable way to get to and from the job offered; (4) make sure that the job offered is at a safe and healthy place and provides workman's compensation; and (5) give the father an opportunity to explain why he refused the job offer.[52]

What constitutes past employment for the purpose of receiving ADCU?

There are two usual ways of showing a work history: (1) a father may show that sometime during the four years before applying for ADCU, he did "six quarters of work." A "quarter of work" is the three-month period in which the father worked and earned at least fifty dollars or participated in a work-training program;[53] or (2) if the father receives unemployment compensation, the family is automatically entitled to ADCU if the unemployment benefits are not enough to meet their needs.

How long can a family continue to receive ADCU?

ADCU payments will continue for as long as the family needs them. But the father will be required to continue to look for work and to participate in the Work Incentive Program. See p. 53.

---

[52]45 C.F.R. §233.100(a)(3)(ii).

[53]The 1st quarter is January, February, March; the 2nd is April, May, June; the 3rd is July, August, September, the 4th is October, November, December. See 45 C.F.R. §233.100(a)(3)(iii)&(iv).

Is ADCU available when the father is on strike?

Yes, in all but a few states. Some courts have held that if a state provides ADCU benefits, it cannot refuse to pay them simply because the father is out of work because of a labor dispute.[54] The Nixon administration has issued new regulations saying that states are free to decide whether or not they will pay ADCU to strikers, and these regulations have not yet been tested in court.[55]

Is ADCU available to families headed by men?

Yes. Since 98% of the families receiving ADC are headed by women, this booklet refers to mothers and fathers in traditional roles.

A male-headed family may receive regular ADC if the mother is dead, absent from the home, *or* disabled.

ADCU is available only when the *father* is unemployed. This discrimination may be unconstitutional. If a family needs aid because the mother, who has a work history, loses her job and the father has been caring for the children, the family should seek help from a lawyer.

AMOUNT OF WELFARE PAYMENTS

How are welfare grants computed?

To figure out how much a welfare grant should be, the caseworker first adds up the amount of money allowed by the department to cover a family's *regular needs* such as

---

[54]*Davidson v. Francis,* 340 F.Supp. 351 (D. Md. 1972), aff'd. 409 U.S. 904 (1972). *Lascaris v. Wyman,* 328 NYS2d 289 (N.Y. 1972).
[55]45 C.F.R. §233.100.

food and clothing. The amount allowed for each item is
based on the number of people in the family and the
category of aid they receive. Rent may be included on this
list or it may be computed separately. Some states pay the
full rent; others just give a fixed amount for shelter. Any
regular income which the family has is subtracted from
the amount allowed to provide for the family's regular
needs. The remaining sum is known as the *regular
recognized need*. In some states the amount of the grant
is the same as the recognized need. In other states the
grant is only a portion of the recognized need.

This sounds simple, but usually it is not. Figuring out
the correct grant is especially difficult when someone in
the family is working, other people live with the family,
the family receives support payments, or the state does
not pay full need.

Who decides what a family's needs are?

When welfare administrators talk about what a person
or family "needs" to live they do not mean the amount of
money people actually require to live a decent life. In
July 1971, the United States Department of Labor said
that to live decently an urban family of four needs at
least $7214 a year or $601 a month. If you look at the
chart at the back of the book, you will see that no state
in America pays that much to families on welfare. The
National Welfare Rights Organization has sponsored
legislation that would pay people what the Department of
Labor says they really need, but it is not likely to pass
in the near future. Therefore, when the welfare caseworker
computes your grant, he or she is simply adding up the
amount of money that the welfare department has decided
it will provide to pay for the things a family needs. That
money will not be enough to live decently.

How do you know if you are getting the full amount allowed by the department?

Most welfare departments have a chart showing the amounts of money allowed for different items in the various categories of welfare. You are also entitled to have a written statement of how your welfare grant is figured out, and you should not hesitate to demand one since caseworkers often make mistakes. You should ask the caseworker to explain how the grant was computed, and you should also ask a friend or a welfare-rights worker who knows the rules and is good with numbers to make sure you are getting the correct amount of money.

What are the regular needs that welfare provides for?

Besides the basic needs for food, clothing, and shelter some states recognize that some people have special requirements on a regular day-to-day basis. Some of the most commonly recognized special needs are: special diets for pregnant mothers and sick people; extra allowances for utilities; extra allowances for people who are old, disabled, or blind; extra money for people who have no kitchens and must eat in restaurants; transportation allowances to go to the doctor for regular appointments; money for a telephone for people who are sick or isolated; expenses for work or for education. No state gives money for all of these things. Some states do not recognize any of them. But you should ask your caseworker, or, even better, a welfare-rights worker, whether money for any of these special regular needs is granted to people in your state.

See page 43 for information on grants for special needs which arise on an irregular basis, and ideas on how to get and keep special needs grants.

What is regular income?

In deciding how much you need, welfare will look at all of the money that you get regularly. This includes money from work, money from support payments, un-employment-compensation payments, Social Security benefits, and rent or other money you get regularly from a boarder. This income must be regularly and actually available to spend.

The basic federal rule is that "only such net income as is actually available for current use on a regular basis will be considered."[56] The welfare department cannot count as "regular income" money that is merely promised or owed to you. Until you have the cash in hand it does not count. The welfare department cannot count money given to you for a specific purpose, such as money earned under a work-study program which you need to stay in school.[56A] "On a regular basis" means that welfare cannot count irregular gifts or contributions from friends or relatives in determining the grant.

The welfare department also cannot assume that someone is contributing to a family's income just because he is supposed to be or because he is living with the family. There are three common situations in which welfare departments frequently try to make this assumption and thereby cut a family's grant.

Stepfathers. A man is legally obligated to support himself, his wife, and his own children. Stepfathers are not obligated to give a single penny for the support of the children of another man. Neither are friends or lovers. If a stepfather or any other man voluntarily chooses to support children who aren't his own on a regular basis (as opposed to occasional gift-giving), these contributions are income and will be considered in determining the welfare grant, but the welfare department can't simply as-

---
[56] 45 C.F.R. 233.20(a)(3)(ii)
[56A] *Brown v. Bates,* 363 F.Supp. 897 (N.D. Ohio 1973).

sume a man is making such contributions, even though he is living in the house and supporting his wife and his own children.

The welfare department can deduct the stepfather's payments for rent, food, and expenses for himself, his wife, and his own children from the welfare grant only if he is actually making such payments. Remember, only income actually available for current use on a regular basis can be considered.[57]

Absent fathers. Absent fathers, just like fathers who live at home, are required to support their children. This, of course, does not necessarily mean that they always do so, and when they don't many women ask a court to order them to. Frequently, the welfare department tries to tell these women that because a support order was issued, their welfare will be cut off. This is illegal. A support order will not feed a family and unless the money is actually being received from the absent father, his family's welfare cannot be terminated.

Support payments can be used only for the wife and children of the man who pays them. So if Mrs. B. has two children by Mr. B. and two more children by Mr. A., Mr. B.'s support payments go only to her and his children. Welfare must pay the full needs for Mr. A.'s children.[58]

If there is only one child in the family, and that child is receiving support payments which are large enough to meet his or her needs, the question comes up whether the mother is entitled to welfare. The mother must receive aid because ADC is a program for families, including the

[57]*Lewis v. Martin*, 397 U.S. 552 (1970), *Solman v. Shapiro*, 300 F.Supp. 409 (D. Conn.), aff'd, 396 U.S. 5 (1969), *Boucher v. Minter*, 349 F.Supp. 1240 (D. Mass. 1972). See also, *Jenkins v. Georges*, 312 F.Supp. 289 (W.D. Pa. 1969), *Owens v. Parham*, 350 F. Supp. 598 (N.D. Ga. 1972), *Rosen v. Hursh*, 464 F.2d 731 (8th Cir. 1972).
[58]*Gilliard v. Craig*, 331 F.Supp. 587 (W.D. N.C. 1971), *Bourque v. Conn. Comm. of Welfare*, 2 CCH Pov. L. Rpt. ¶15,537 (Conn. Cir. Ct. App. Div., 1972), *Dorsey v. State Dept. of Social Services*, 292 A.2d 60, (Md. Ct. of App. 1972).

caretaker, and because two people cannot live as cheaply as one at subsistence level.[59]

In some places absent fathers make support payments directly to the welfare department which in turn issues a check to his family. This is usually a good system for most families because it means that even if the father misses a payment, his family still gets its check from the welfare department.

If you are supposed to receive support payments directly from your husband and he does not send a check, you should tell your caseworker and demand that the grant be increased.[60]

Boarders. Boarders and roomers are not counted as members of the household in determining the amount of a family's grant, but any money that they regularly pay for room and board is deducted from the grant as income.

The income of a person living in a household who does not receive assistance cannot be counted as income in determining a family's grant unless the family is actually receiving money regularly from the person.[61] For example, if there is a sixteen-year-old cousin in the family who is working, his income cannot be used to lower the grant unless he actually contributes to the support of the household.

The welfare department will often deduct this person's "share" of the rent from your grant. If this happens and you are not actually receiving rent money, you should contact a welfare-rights worker or a lawyer.

Is all money that a family receives counted as income?

In many states, the welfare department will allow the recipient to keep some of the income from whatever source.

[59]*Rodriquez v. Vowell*, 742 F.2d 622 (5th Cir. 1972), cert. denied, 935. Ct. 2777 (1973).

[60]45 C.F.R. §233.20(a)(3)(v).

[61]*Hurley v. Van Lare*, 365 F.Supp. 186 (S.D. N.Y. 1973). *Mothers & Children's Organization v. Stanton*, — F.Supp. — (N.D. Ind. 1973).

This income will not be looked at in deciding how much the family needs. For example, many states disregard the first five dollars of each individual's income from any source. So if Mrs. A. receives fifty dollars a month in support from Mr. A. for herself and Mr. A.'s two children, welfare can only count thirty-five dollars in determining how much the family needs, since it must disregard five dollars each for Mr. A. and the two children, or a total of fifteen dollars.

In addition to these disregards for any sort of income, there are special rules for disregarding money earned by working. These are described on page 62.

What property are people on welfare allowed to own?

In every state the welfare department allows people to keep basic personal property while receiving them aid. Personal property includes clothes, furniture, dishes and kitchen utensils, record players, radios, and televisions. Most states also allow people to continue living in the same place they lived before they went on welfare. Cars are usually allowed in rural areas. In some places small life insurance policies and savings accounts are permitted. The major allowable resources for people on welfare in all of the states are listed in the chart at the back of the book.

The actual availability rule also applies to property. You can't be denied welfare because you have a rich uncle who might die some day and leave you a lot of money. You can't be denied welfare because you are allowed to live in the house of a relative. If the house is not yours to sell, welfare can't force you to sell it or sign a lien on it. You can't be denied welfare because your children have a trust fund for their future education. If the money in the trust fund is not available to you now, it does not count.

SAMPLE BUDGET FOR NONWORKING FAMILY

Mrs. Smith is the mother of three children. Mr. Smith, the father of all the children, lives apart from the family and sends them fifty dollars a month in support. The oldest child is anemic and needs a special diet. The family pays seventy-five dollars a month for rent.

Step 1: add up the needs. Look at the state's ADC need chart for a family of four. This will vary from state to state. Check whether the state computes rent separately and whether it recognizes special needs.

	Per Month Cost
Basic ADC needs for family of four	$200
Rent	$ 75
Special diet	$ 10
Total needs	$285

Step 2: add up the income actually available. In this case the only income is the fifty dollars a month from Mr. Smith.

Step 3: apply the disregard. Let us assume that in this state, five dollars a month of income from any source is disregarded. Four people are receiving income from the support, so that is five dollars per person or twenty dollars per month.

	Per Month Cost
Income	$50
Minus disregard	$20
Available income	$30

Step 4: figure out recognized need. You simply subtract the available income from the amount needed according to the welfare chart.

	Per Month Cost
Need	$285
Minus available income	$ 30
Unmet need	$255

Step 5: figure out the grant. Unfortunately, many states do not pay the full amount that welfare recognizes as what a family needs to survive. In states that pay full need, the family will receive a grant in the amount of their recognized need. In these states the Smith family would get $255 a month. Other states impose maximums on the amount of aid that may be paid. There are three basic sorts of maximums.

Family maximum. Some states say no family may receive more than a certain amount of welfare money no matter how many people are in the family. For example, in a state that has a family maximum of two hundred dollars a month, a family of six people will receive two hundred dollars a month and a family of ten will receive exactly the same. A family maximum does not hurt people in small families, but ten people obviously need more to live on than six people do, so in states with a family maximum people in large families have a very difficult time surviving. In fact, many families have been broken up because they have had to send children to live with relatives. The U.S. Supreme Court has held in spite of the obvious hardships caused by the system that it is permissible for states to set family welfare maximums in order to save money.[62]

Percentage maximum. Other states say that a family may receive only a certain percentage of the state-recognized need. For example, if the state pays 50 percent of need, the Smith family will receive $127.50, or half of what the welfare department recognizes that they need.

---

[62]*Dandridge v. Williams,* 397 U.S. 471 (1970).

Dollar maximum. Still other states impose specific dollar limitations on the amount a family can receive. For example, a state may pay twenty-four dollars a month for the first child and twenty dollars a month for each additional child. In this state, the Smith family would receive eighty-four dollars a month, even though that amount would not nearly meet their needs.

Other methods. Finally, some states use combinations of these methods, e.g., ten dollars per child and 20 percent of the unmet need. Some of these methods are so complex that it takes an accountant to figure a welfare budget correctly. Errors are frequently made—generally in favor of the welfare department.

How can a person know if his or her welfare grant has been figured correctly?

Two points should be checked.

Did the welfare department follow its own rules for computing a grant and were its figures computed correctly? This is sometimes difficult to check, but a welfare-rights worker, lawyer, or anyone else who knows the rules and is good at math should be able to help. People should always check how the amount of this grant was arrived at or have someone do it for them. Many people have lost money they were entitled to simply assuming that the welfare department got everything right.

Are the welfare department's rules for figuring out grants legal? Both Congress and the Supreme Court have established certain technical rules which the state welfare departments must follow in giving aid,[63] but lawyers at the Columbia Center on Social Welfare Policy and Law say that in most states these rules are not being followed and

---

[63]*Rosado v. Wyman*, 397 U.S. 397 (1970), (on remand), 322 F.Supp. 1173 (E.D.N.Y. 1970), 437 F.2d 619 (2nd Cir. 1970), *aff'd. per curiam*, 402 U.S. 991 (1971). *Jefferson v. Hackney*, 397 U.S. 821 (1970), (on remand) 304 F.Supp. 1332 (N.D. Tex. 1969).

welfare grants are being computed illegally. Lawsuits are needed to force these welfare departments to comply with the law.

How can someone get a grant to meet special needs?

Special grants are available in some states for special needs. You obtain a special-need grant in these states simply by asking for one and showing that you need it. Some examples of the special needs provided for by different states are grants for school expenses in Arkansas,[64] grants for the replacement of household furnishings destroyed by fire or other disaster in New York,[65] and grants for laundry, telephone, and transportation in Wisconsin. All states that have Medicaid programs are required to pay special grants for transportation to people who need to travel to receive necessary medical care.[66]

If you do not know whether there are special grants available in your state, don't simply rely on what a caseworker tells you. Go to a lawyer or a welfare-rights worker and have that person look up the law. Occasionally special grants are provided for in laws other than the welfare law. For example, in some places education laws provide for special grants for clothing and supplies for school children.

If a state was making payments for special needs in 1968, it cannot stop making such payments unless it positively shows that people no longer need the items.[67] It is difficult to imagine an item which people needed in 1968, which they no longer need now. In the past

---

[64]Arkansas Public Assistance Manual, §2322.3 provides $4 extra a month for each child regularly attending school.

[65]N.Y. Social Services Law, §131a(6); 18 N.Y.C.R.R. §352.7 (d).

[66]45 C.F.R. §249.10(a)(5).

[67]*Rosado v. Wyman,* 397 U.S. 397 (1970), [on remand] 322 F.Supp. 1173 (E.D.N.Y. 1970), 437 F.2d 619 (2nd Cir. 1970), *aff'd per curiam,* 402 U.S. 991 (1971).

few years many states have simplified the method by which they compute welfare grants and have incorporated special-need grants into the regular welfare grant. The states may do this, but they must do it in a way that is statistically fair. If the department of welfare stops making payment for a special-need item which they used to provide, you should see a lawyer.

In the past, campaigns by welfare recipients have been successful in forcing welfare departments to provide for particular needs that were common to a large number of people. Although today with the increasing pressure to cut welfare it is more difficult to win by demonstrating, in some cases it may still be the best thing to do.

OTHER RIGHTS AND DUTIES OF WELFARE RECIPIENTS

Do you have to pay back welfare if you get enough money to do so?

Almost every state requires that you pay welfare back for everything you have received if you get enough money at some later time in your life. Some states require that you give the welfare department a lien on any property that you own at the time you apply for aid. A lien means that the welfare department can sell the property and keep the money, if you later have enough money to pay them back but refuse to do so. The welfare department can make you sign a lien before you begin receiving aid.[68]

In collecting back the money they have paid you, welfare should not: (1) take any money from your wages; (2) force you to give up the house you live in; (3) take so much money that you do not have enough left to live decently;

---

[68]*Charleston v. Wohlgemuth*, 332 F.Supp. 1175 (E.D. Pa. 1971), *aff'd* 405 U.S. 970 (1972). *Fitzpatrick v. Illinois Dept. of Public Aid*, 52 Ill. 2d 218, N.E. 666 (1972).

(4) take lump sum social security benefits;[69] or (5) take
so much money that you are forced to go back on welfare.[70]

The legal rules for recovery of welfare benefits are unclear. If welfare is trying to collect money from you and
you do not have enough both to pay them and live
decently, you should see a lawyer. As a matter of practice,
welfare is most likely to try to collect for money they
have paid you when you: (1) inherit money or get money
on an insurance policy; (2) win the lottery; or (3) win a
lawsuit and get money for a personal injury. In many
places, if you are injured the welfare department will make
you sign a paper in advance so that they can collect any
money that you might get from a personal-injury lawsuit.

A welfare recipient who gets a large sum of money
in one of the above ways should immediately tell his caseworker that he no longer wants to receive aid. Once he
has stopped receiving welfare he is free to spend the
money he got in any way and as quickly as he pleases—
buy something he has always needed or wanted. The
money is his and it is not illegal to spend it. In fact, if
he does not spend the money, welfare may try to collect
it from him for past assistance paid. The welfare recipient
can fight this (he'll need a lawyer) by showing that if he
pays back the welfare department he will again be forced
into poverty, but it is much easier and better for him if he
just spends it. Either way he will end up back on welfare,
but at least if he spent the money instead of paying it
back he will have something that he needs and wants.

**What should a welfare recipient do if his economic
circumstances change for the better?**

Welfare rules require that recipients of aid report to the

[69]*Philpott v. Essex Co. Welfare Board*, 409 U.S. 413 (1973).
[70]*Snell v. Wyman*, 281 F. Supp. 853 (S.D. N.Y. 1968), *aff'd*
393 U.S. 323 (1969).

department if they get a job or begin receiving any other kind of regular income. They must also report to the department any other change of circumstances that might affect the amount of a grant, such as a child leaving home.

Can the welfare department reduce your grant because of a previous "overpayment"?

Sometimes the welfare department makes mistakes and pays a person more money than he is supposed to get. At other times, the recipient gives the caseworker the wrong information, and gets extra money.

The law in this area is in a state of change. Until 1973 the federal law limited the circumstances in which the department of welfare could deduct previous overpayments from current welfare grants. In 1973 the Nixon administration reinterpreted the Social Security Act to allow reductions in current welfare grants where the family had received an overpayment, either because of the mistake of the department or because of fraud.[71] The new Nixon regulations give the states a choice and allow each state to decide whether they want to expand the circumstances in which current grants will be reduced to recover for previous overpayment. It is not now clear which states will take this option and begin reducing grants. Furthermore, poor people have filed suit saying that the new Nixon regulations are an illegal interpretation of the Social Security Act.[72] The courts have not yet decided whether or not the new regulations are legal.

What were the federal rules on reducing welfare grants to recover overpayments prior to the Nixon regulations?

Where the welfare department plans to terminate or re-

[71]45 C.F.R. §233.20(a)(12).
[72]National Welfare Rights Organization v. Weinberger, D.C.D.C. filed Sept. 5, 1973, Civ. No. 1703-73.

duce a grant because of past overpayment or fraud the law specifies no termination for past fraud or overpayment. The current welfare grant can never be cut off completely, even if the department proves that the recipient acted dishonestly.

Grant reduction is permitted only if recipient still has extra money. The current grant can be reduced if the recipient still has the money which he was "overpaid." This is not very likely to happen because welfare grants are so low, whenever a poor family gets "too much" money they are likely to spend it right away.

There are no reductions if recipient was honest. Current grants can *never be reduced* for past overpayment if the recipient was honest but the department made a mistake.[73] (If you still have the extra money, you may be required to give it back.)

Reasonable reductions are permitted for proven fraud. In most states, current grants can be reduced for past fraud if the welfare department has evidence "which clearly established that a recipient willfully withheld information about his income or resources."[74]

"Willfully" means that the recipient acted dishonestly and *knew* at the time that he was acting dishonestly. The department must *prove* that the recipient was willfully dishonest. In a case where the department alleges that the recipient withheld information, or failed to report income, there are many factors which would tend to show that the recipient was not willful. For example:

(1.) The recipient may remember that he reported the income to the caseworker. Caseworkers are not perfect and sometimes forget things they are told.

(2.) The recipient may have reported the income to someone else—for example, the unemployment office—and believed that that was enough.

(3.) The recipient may believe that the caseworker knew about the income without being told directly. For example,

[73]45 C.F.R. §233.20(a)(3)(ii)(c).
[74]45 C.F.R. §233.20(a)(3)(ii)(d).

if the caseworker helped to make child care arrangements so the mother could work.

(4.) The recipient may believe that it was unnecessary to report the income, e.g., because the worker was young or the income was irregular.

If the department proves that the recipient willfully concealed income, then past overpayment may be considered in determining present need. The law does not tell us exactly how past "overpayments may reduce current needs," but it does require that "income and resources will be reasonably evaluated."[75]

In at least two states, Pennsylvania and Michigan, courts have held that a family's grant cannot be reduced, including where the recipient has been convicted of fraud, if the family is currently in need.[76] The reasoning behind these decisions is that past illegality has nothing to do with present need and in the case of AFDC innocent children should not be punished for the crimes of their parents.

Sometimes welfare recipients sign "repayment agreements" accepting a reduction in grant. For example, the welfare department may pay back rent or utility bills to prevent eviction or the cutoff of electricity. At other times the welfare department may issue a duplicate of a check that was lost or stolen. When the welfare department pays this "extra" money they sometimes ask a recipient to sign an agreement to pay the department back out of future welfare grants. If it is impossible for you and your family to live decently on the reduced grant, the repayment agreement may be illegal.[77] You should see a lawyer. Even though you have signed a repayment agreement, you must be given the right to a fair hearing before your grant is reduced.[78]

[75]45 C.F.R. 233.20(a)(3)(ii)(e).

[76]*Cooper v. Laupheimer*, 316 F.Supp. 26 (E.D. Pa. 1970), *Bradford v. Juras*, 331 F.Supp. 167, (D. Ore. 1971), *Evans v. Dept. of Social Service*, 22 Mich. App. 633 (1970).

[77]*In re R.S.*, 2 CCH Pov. L. Rpt. ¶15,115 (N.Y. Dept. of Soc. Serv. 1970).

[78]*Hagans v. Wyman*, —— F.Supp. —— (E.D.N.Y. 1972),

What are the Nixon regulations for the reduction of current grants because of past overpayments?

The state may recover any overpayment, even those made as a result of welfare department error.

Except in cases where there is evidence which clearly establishes that the recipient willfully withheld information, recoupment must be limited to overpayments made during the twelve months preceding the month in which the overpayment was discovered.

If recoupment is made through reduction in the current assistance grant, "The state shall establish reasonable limits on the proportion of such payments that may be deducted, so as not to cause undue hardship on recipients."[79]

Since welfare recipients experience great hardship even when receiving full grants it is difficult to know how grants can be reduced so as not to cause undue hardship.

What rules must the welfare department follow in investigating welfare recipients?

Welfare fraud is a crime in every state, punishable by a fine or prison sentence. You can only be punished for welfare fraud, however, if it is proven in a court of law that you cheated deliberately. The welfare department has no power to put people in jail or fine them. All it can do is bring charges against a person, who then has a right to regular trial just as he would if he were accused of any other crime.

---

2 CCH Pov. L. Rpt. ¶16,323, reversed on other grounds, ——— F2d ———, cert. granted. ——— U.S. ——— (1973). Under the new HEW fair hearing regulations a recipient may only be entitled to notice, at the time of reduction of aid, and a subsequent hearing to challenge the reduction. 45 C.F.R. §205.10 (a)(4)(ii)(B).

[79] 45 C.F.R. §233.20(a)(12)(i)(D).

It is worth noting here that available statistics show that welfare recipients cheat less than other people. In 1969, for example, a federal government investigation of fraud showed that only four out of every one thousand welfare cases were fraudulent[80] while figures on national tax fraud and evasion were much higher. Farmers, small businessmen, and professionals together fail to report 28 percent of their total income. Receivers of interest fail to report 34 percent of their income and people receiving rent, royalties, and capital gains don't report 11 percent of their income.[81]

In spite of these facts, welfare departments have investigated welfare recipients' claims more thoroughly than the Internal Revenue Service investigates tax frauds.

Until 1973 there were federal rules which sought to assure "full respect for the rights and dignity of applicants for, and recipients of assistance."[82] These rules required that the recipient or applicant be the primary source of information about eligibility for welfare, and that the welfare department obtain the specific consent of the individual before contacting other people such as landlords, neighbors, relatives, and former employees.[83] Even though these rules were often violated by the welfare department, they were important in helping to assure decent treatment for the poor. Now the Nixon administration has said that the states may abolish these rules which protect poor people from abusive investigatory practices.[84]

The welfare department must still respect the constitutional rights of welfare recipients. For example, the department cannot conduct "unreasonable searches," such as a

---

[80]HEW, Social and Rehabilitation Service, "Selected Data About Public Welfare," Sept. 1969.

[81]Stern, Philip M., The Great Treasury Raid, Random House (New York: 1965).

[82]45 C.F.R. §205.20. Revoked eff. Oct. 15, 1973, 38 Fed. Reg. 22008, (Aug. 15, 1973).

[83]45 C.F.R. §206.10(a)(12). Revised eff. Oct. 15, 1973, 38 Fed. Reg. 22009, (Aug. 15, 1973).

[84]38 Fed. Reg. 22005, (Aug. 15, 1973).

search at five o'clock in the morning. However the Supreme Court has said that compulsory home visits do not violate constitutional rights, even though in most cases all of the relevant information could be obtained at the welfare office.[85]

Do welfare recipients have a right to receive cash benefits?

Yes. A basic rule and right of the federal welfare programs is that payments must be made in cash to be spent as the recipient sees fit.

There are two exceptions to this rule. In these special cases, the welfare check will be given as a "third party" or "vendor" payment. A third-party check is a check to some responsible person who will then see that the family is taken care of. A vendor check is a check directly to the landlord, grocer, etc. Welfare can be given in vendor or third-party checks only when the person receiving the cash grant refuses without good cause to participate in the Work Incentive Program,[86] or is proven to be unable to manage money and the welfare money is not being used to take care of the children.[87]

If your check is a third-party or vendor check because of mismanagement, welfare must make special efforts to help you learn to manage money and to overcome the problems you are facing.[88]

If welfare wants to make vendor or third-party payments, they must give you a fair hearing to challenge whether the check should be restricted or to challenge the selection of the person who will receive the check for the family.[89]

---

[85]*Wyman v. James,* 400 U.S. 309 (1971).

[86]42 U.S.C. §602(a)(19)(F).

[87]45 C.F.R. §234.60(a)(2).

[88]45 C.F.R. §234.60(a)(8).

[89]45 C.F.R. §§234.60(a)(11), and 205.10(a)(12)(ii)(C), as amended 38 Fed. Reg. 22008, Aug. 15, 1973. *Cable v. Johnson,* 2 CCH Pov. L. Rpt. 16,245 (E.D. Ky. 1972).

Do you have a right to have the information which you give to the welfare department kept confidential?

Yes. All of the information you give to the welfare department is confidential. They should not give this information to any other people or agencies, without your specific permission.[90]

---

[90]45 C.F.R. §205.50(a)(6). New regulations would allow the welfare department to release information about adult recipients (Aged, Blind, or Disabled) to other public officials under specific conditions. 38 Fed. Reg. 22141, (Aug. 16, 1973).

II

Work Requirements

What is the Work Incentive Program?

In 1967 the federal government passed a law requiring every state to establish a Work Incentive Program (WIN) which would place welfare recipients in jobs or provide them with job training, including schooling. Since then, each state has selected the areas with the most people and highest rate of unemployment in which to establish the program. People on the program receive a reduced welfare grant and are allowed to keep part of their earnings. (See pages 54–55.)

Can anyone on welfare join a WIN program?

Only people who live in an area in which a WIN program has been set up can join. Even many people who live in an area in which there is a program can't get in because there are simply not enough jobs and training positions to go around. Lawsuits brought to force the state to begin a program in a new area have not been successful.[1] However, negotiations with welfare officials might cause them to set up a new program.

---

[1] *See Calexico Welfare Rights Organization v. Sheffield*, Civ. No. C-70-1370, Complaint filed U.S. Dist. Court, N.D. Calif. 1970.

Who must register for work or training?

In December 1971 Congress passed a law which requires almost all able-bodied adults to register for work to continue getting ADC. This law went into operation on July 1, 1972. Under it all ADC recipients must register for work except: (1) children under sixteen, or under twenty-one and in school; (2) people who are ill, incapacitated, or elderly; (3) people who are required to care for a sick or incapacitated member of the household; (4) mothers with children under six years old; (5) women who care for children and who have a male relative in the household who has not refused to register for work; and (6) people who would need to travel more than one hour to reach a work project.

The welfare department decides whether you are "appropriate" to register for work. If the department decides you should register for work and you believe that you should not have to register, you should request a fair hearing. Fair hearings and the penalties for refusing to register are discussed on page 57.

What sorts of jobs and training are available under the WIN program?

There are three kinds of jobs or training available under WIN: (1) jobs or on-the-job training in the regular economy; (2) special training programs established under the WIN program; and (3) public-service jobs.

How much money can a welfare recipient earn and keep in a WIN job.[2]

A job or job training in the regular economy must pay you at least the minimum wage, if applicable, or a higher

---

[2] 45 C.F.R. §233.20.

wage if other workers in the area usually make more money doing the same work. In no case can you be forced to take a regular job which pays less than three fourths of the federal minimum wage, or $1.20 per hour in industrial work, and $.97 an hour for agricultural work. If you get a job in the regular economy you must be allowed to keep the first $30.00 of your monthly wages and one third of the balance. This $30.00 and one third of the balance must be disregarded in determining your need for welfare. You must also be allowed child care and work expenses. A sample budget for a welfare recipient with a regular job is presented on page 62.

In a special training program under the WIN program you must continue to receive your full welfare grant, plus reimbursement for child care and work expenses, plus a thirty-dollar-a-month incentive payment.

In public-service employment you must earn at least the minimum wage, if applicable, or a higher wage if other workers normally make more for doing the same work. Child care and work expenses must be considered in determining whether you still need welfare. Public service workers are not entitled to have the first thirty dollars plus one third of the balance of their income disregarded in determining their need for welfare.

What rights do people assigned to the WIN program have?

Medical examination. No one can be assigned to a WIN program without first having been given a full medical examination to make sure that they are strong enough to work.

Job interview. After the medical examination a WIN-program participant is entitled to an interview with a worker in the state labor department or employment service to find out what sort of work or training he or she wants to do and can do best.

Adequate child-care arrangements. Before a mother can be sent to the WIN program or to work, there must be an adequate plan for the care of her children. If the children stay at home, there must be a responsible adult who is in good health and able to take care of them. If children are in school there must be someone to watch them when they get home. If the children are to be cared for at some- one else's home or at a day-care center, they should not have to change schools and their mother should not need to travel out of her way to leave them off or pick them up. Child-care arrangements must be suitable for the in- dividual child. Where there is a choice of child-care ar- rangements, the mother must be allowed to decide.[3] You can make your own plans for child care and welfare must allow your expenses as an additional need.

Refusal to participate in WIN or take a job for "good cause." All of the following reasons are "good cause" to refuse work under WIN.[4] If you have "good cause" to refuse you can do so without reduction in the grant or penalty of any sort.

(1.) It takes too long to commute from home to work. In no case should the total commuting time per day be more than two hours and, in the case of mothers, commut- ing time should be much less.

(2.) Inadequate provision made for medical care or ser- vices necessary for participation in the program.

(3.) The job offer is not for a specific job at a stated wage.

(4.) The job does not pay enough.

(5.) The job is available because of a labor dispute. Welfare recipients cannot be forced to do scab labor.

(6.) The job is too difficult for you. If you do not have the physical, mental, or emotional capacity to do the job well, you have "good cause" to refuse it.

(7.) Acceptance of the job or training would be un-

---

[3] 45 C.F.R. 220.18.
[4] Dept. of Labor, WIN Handbook §412 (E).

reasonable because it would interrupt your own plans to go back to your regular work.

(8.) Acceptance of the assignment would be bad for economic welfare of the individual or the family.

(9.) Acceptance of the assignment would disrupt family life.

(10.) Acceptance of the assignment would be dangerous to the health or safety of you or your family.

(11.) The working conditions are not safe or healthy or the hours are longer than are usual for a job of that nature.

(12.) Workmen's compensation insurance is not provided for on the job.

What happens when a WIN participant disagrees with the decision of a welfare worker about his case?

WIN participants have a right to a hearing when disagreements arise with welfare officials about their cases at any point in the process. Your grant cannot be terminated or reduced without a written notice of the reasons for the proposed action and a prior hearing on request. For example, you are entitled to a hearing when: (1) you want to be referred to WIN but the department of welfare refuses to refer you; (2) the department wants to refer you to WIN, or make you register for work, but you think that you are not an appropriate person for work registration; (3) the department of labor wants to assign you to a particular job, but you think you have good cause to refuse that assignment; and (4) you have taken a job and want to quit and think that you have good cause to do so. These are examples of situations in which fair hearings are frequently requested, but you are entitled to a hearing any time any dispute arises between you and the department about your case.[5]

---

[5]29 C.F.R. §57.1, as amended 37 Fed. Reg. 14268 (July 18, 1972).

What happens to people who refuse to work or who quit their jobs?

When a WIN counselor thinks that you have refused or quit work or training without "good cause," he will send you a written notice which should describe what you were asked to do, your reasons for refusal, and the counselor's reasons that these were not considered "good cause." The notice must also tell you how you can get a fair hearing. *Within seven days after this notice is mailed to you, you must request a fair hearing. If you do not make this request within seven days, welfare will be notified and the grant may be reduced.*

You should request a hearing with a letter explaining all the reasons that you do not want to work or to take the job or training that you have been offered. (You also may request a review by telling your counselor, but it is better to write a letter.) Your rights in welfare fair hearings are described on page 72.

The state may provide for an appeal from the fair-hearing decision. If you lose the fair hearing, and if your state provides for an appeal, you should take that appeal. You should consult a lawyer or a welfare-rights worker to find out what the appeal rights are in your state.

After the decision of the state fair-hearing appeals board (or after the fair-hearing decision if the state has no appeals process), you can request a review by the Department of Labor National Review Panel. This review must be requested within fifteen days of the fair hearing, or fair-hearing appeals decision. In most cases the National Review Panel will make its decision on the basis of the facts presented at the fair hearing and will not conduct another hearing. The National Review Panel does not have to consider every case, but rather only considers those cases that raise some important question. If the National Review Panel decides not to consider your case, or decides against you, you will be notified.

Your welfare grant cannot be reduced while any of these appeals and reviews are still going on.

What happens if you refuse to register for work or to accept a job and you lose all your hearings and appeals?

Counseling. First, you are entitled to sixty days of counseling to persuade you that you should accept work. If you are willing to accept this counseling, your grant will continue for sixty days. The sixty days of counseling begin when the time for appeal has expired and you have not filed an appeal, or after a final decision of the National Review Board which is adverse to you.[6] Even though your grant may not be reduced during this counseling period, the department of welfare may pay your grant in the form of a restricted two-party check. (For example, the rent money may be paid directly to the landlord and the utilities directly to the electric company.)

During this sixty-day period you can decide to register for work or accept the job offered to you and there will be no penalty. You are not entitled to the sixty days of counseling if you have refused to register or refused a job without good cause at some earlier time.

Penalties. When the counseling period is over, the following penalties may be imposed on people who refuse to register for work or to take a job that is offered.

(1.) If the person refusing is the person who receives the check for the family, his or her needs will no longer be taken into account in determining the amount of the grant. The law says that restricted two-party checks should be issued for the rest of the family. It is easy enough to issue restricted checks for rent and utilities. It is not so easy for the walfare department to issue restricted checks for groceries and other needs. Unless there is another adult in the family the person refusing work will probably

---

[6]29 C.F.R. §57.12, as amended 37 Fed. Reg. 14270 (July 18, 1972), 45 C.F.R. §220.35(a)(7) and (8).

continue to receive the family check, but it will be reduced by the amount which would otherwise go to the person who has refused work.

(2.) If the only child in the family refuses to work, the ADC grant will be terminated and the rest of the family may get general assistance.

(3.) If one child in a family that has other children refuses to go to an interview, his needs will no longer be included in determining the amount of the grant, but there will be no restriction.

(4.) If a relative who is not the person receiving the check refuses an interview, his needs will no longer be taken into consideration in determining the grant.

People who are not required to work but volunteer to do so and then quit are not subject to these penalties.[7]

Can you reapply for assistance after you have been terminated for refusing work?

Yes, but you must wait ninety days and you must be willing to participate in WIN. If you are reaccepted for welfare and again refuse to register for work or accept a job, you must wait six months before you will be accepted for a third time.[8]

Can the WIN program favor men over women in assigning jobs?

The welfare department will refer people to available jobs and training positions in the following order: unemployed fathers, volunteer mothers, other mothers and pregnant women under nineteen, dependent children and relatives over sixteen, and all others.

If a woman wants a job or job-training, this order of referral discriminates against her. Theoretically, a volun-

---

[7]45 C.F.R. §233.11(F)(3)(ii).
[8]29 C.F.R. §57.13.

teering mother cannot get a job or a training position until all of the unemployed fathers have been assigned, whether the men want work or not. One court has held that this discrimination against women is illegal, even though the cost of child care means that it is more expensive for the state to provide a job to a woman than to a man.[9] If there is a WIN program in your area but you cannot get a job or training position through it, you should see a lawyer.

Can a welfare recipient go to college under the WIN program?

Sometimes. Under the WIN program, the welfare department decides who is "appropriate" for work or training and then refers these people to the state labor department. The labor department counsels the individual and helps work out a plan that includes college education. If the labor department works out such a plan, the welfare department must pay welfare, work, and child-care expenses.[10]

If you receive welfare, and you want to go to college, you should not depend upon the welfare department or the labor department to help you get there. If you make your own plans for going to college, and enroll, the welfare department may try to terminate your grant or refuse to give you child-care and work expenses. A court in New York has said that the welfare department must allow recipients to go to college if that is the work they choose, and must pay assistance and child-care expenses.[11] On the other hand, a court in Pennsylvania held that a law student could not continue receiving assistance for himself

---

[9]*Thorn v. Richardson*, —— F.Supp. —— (W.D. Wash. 1971), 2 CCH, Pov. L. Rpt. ¶1405.55.

[10]*Milwaukee Co. v. Wisc. Dept. of Health and Soc. Services*, 2 CCH Pov. L. Rpt. ¶1405.20 (Wis. Cir. Ct. 1971). See also *Brown v. Bates*, 363 F.Supp. 897 (N.D. Ohio 1973).

[11]*Jefferies v. Sugarman*, 345 F.Supp. 172 (S.D.N.Y. 1972).

and his family because he was not available for work.[12] If you want to go to college, you should see a lawyer to help you to continue receiving welfare.

What is the ADC work incentive and who is entitled to receive it?

Anyone in a family receiving ADC who begins working at a regular job is entitled to have the first thirty dollars a month and one third of the balance of their gross income disregarded in determining their need for assistance.[13] They are also entitled to receive a welfare allowance for expenses incident to employment. Such expenses include child care, transportation, special clothing or supplies, lunch money, union dues, taxes, and social security. These provisions apply to *everyone* who has received ADC in the past four months, whether they got their job through the WIN program or in any other way. You cannot get the ADC work incentive if you have not received welfare in the past four months, if you quit a better-paying job within the last month in order to get on welfare, or if you deliberately lower your income in the last month to become eligible for welfare.[14]

SAMPLE BUDGET FOR A WORKING ADC RECIPIENT

A mother and her three children have been receiving a total welfare check of $200 per month. The mother

---

[12]*Palmer v. Pennsylvania Dept. of Pub. Welfare*, 5 Pa. Cmwlth. 407, 291 A.2d 313 (1972).

[13]42 USC §602(a)(8).

[14]This rule denies the work incentive, child care and work expenses to workers who earn just a little more than the welfare definition of need but who have not received aid in the past four months. It is unfair but legal. *Conner v. Finch*, 314 F.Supp. 364 (N.D. Ill. 1970) *aff'd per curiam*, 400 U.S. 1003 (1971).

gets a job at which she earns $340 per month, but her take-home pay is only $300 after her boss takes out $40 for taxes and social security. The mother must pay $50 per month to a babysitter, $25 per month for lunches, and $16 per month for transportation.

Step 1: Needs

	Per Month Cost
Amount of the old grant	$200
Expenses for employment	
Babysitter	$50
Lunch	$25
Transportation	$16
Total needs	$281

Step 2: Incentive to Work

Now you must look at the income to figure out the incentive. The pay before taxes is $340. The incentive is $30, plus one third of the balance of the gross income or pay before taxes.

$340   (gross income)

minus $ 30

$310

⅓ of $310=$103

total incentive $ 30

plus $103 (⅓ gross income)

total $133

Step 3:   Add Needs and Incentive

The total needs and the incentive to work should be added together.

$281   (needs)

$133   (incentive)

$414   (total)

Step 4:   Available Income

The income which the mother actually has available is the amount of her *take-home pay*, or $300 in our example.

Step 5:   The New Welfare Grant

          $414   (needs and incentive)
minus $300   (take-home pay)
          ‾‾‾‾‾
          $114   (new welfare grant)

In this example, you can see that, even though the welfare grant is reduced, the family actually has a lot more money to spend.

Before Working	*After Working*
The family had a $200 monthly grant to spend.	The family has:
	$114 from welfare
	$300 take-home pay
	$414 total to spend

What work incentives do children get?

The thirty dollars and one third of the remainder work incentive is only for adult workers in families receiving ADC. There are more generous incentives for children.

If the worker is under twenty-one and (1) a full-time student, or (2) a part-time student who works less than thirty-five hours a week, his *entire salary* is an incentive payment.[15] When a child goes to work, there can be *no* decrease in the family's welfare check. The check should be increased to include allowances for work expenses.

What work expenses must the welfare department allow?

In determining family need for ADC, the welfare department must allow you to deduct any expenses "reasonably attributable" to earning money. This includes travel, taxis, lunches, union dues, special clothing, and equipment needed for work.[16] In addition, the welfare de-

---

[15] 42 U.S.C. §602(a)(8)(A)(i).
[16] 42 U.S.C. §602(a)(7).

partment must disregard scholarships or educational grants which are provided to you to allow you to go to school and which are not available to meet daily living expenses.[17]

Some states have tried to impose a flat limit on the amount of work expenses which will be allowed to ADC recipients, but the courts have said that this is illegal and that all reasonable work expenses must be allowed.[18]

Can a state impose any other work requirements on people receiving ADC?

Yes. Until 1973 the rule was that in areas in which there was a Work Incentive Program, that was the "exclusive manner of applying the carrot and stick," in efforts to place ADC recipients in gainful employment.[19]

In 1973 the U.S. Supreme Court considered the validity of a New York program which imposed work requirements for ADC recipients in addition to those imposed under the Work Incentive Program. Under the New York program all able-bodied adults are required to report to state employment offices every two weeks. If they fail to file a certificate that they have reported to the employment office they are "deemed" to have refused work. The Supreme Court held that states are free to impose work requirements in addition to those in the Work Incentive Program. Further, the Court said that states can deny aid to individuals who fail to comply with the additional state work requirements. The Court did not pass on the

---

[17]45 C.F.R. §233.20(a)(3)(iv).

[18]*Vialpando v. Shea*, 475 F.2d 731 (10th Cir. 1973), —— U.S. —— (1973). *Williford v. Lʳ⌐pheimer*, 311 F.Supp. 720 (E.D. Pa. 1969). *County ⌐f Alameda v. California W.R.O.*, 5 Cal. 3d 730, 488 ⌐ ⌐d 953 (1971), (*en banc*), *appeal dismissed*, 406 U.S. ⌐13 (1972). *Adams v. Parham*, —— F. Supp. —— (Nʳ.⌐. Ga. 1972), 2 CCH Pov. L. Rpt. ¶16,096.

[19]*Woolʄⱴιk v. Brown*, 325 F.Supp. 1162 (E.D. Va. 1971). *Duʟlino v. New York State Dept. of Social Services*, 348 F. Supp. 290, 300 (W.D.N.Y. 1972).

validity of all of the specific provisions of the New York program.[20] This unfortunate decision opens the way for state work programs which lack the protections of the Work Incentive Program.

---

[20]*New York State Department of Social Services v. Dublino,* 409 U.S. 1123 (1973).

III

General Assistance

General Assistance is welfare aid provided by state and local governments to people who do not fit into any of the federal categories. Because the categorical assistance programs are paid for in large part by the federal government the rules governing them are the same throughout the whole country. For example, a fatherless child, no matter where he lives, cannot lose ADC because his mother has a boyfriend. Because general assistance is not a national program like ADC, the rules for its administration may differ in every county or town. In short, the answer to the question, "What are my rights under general assistance?" usually is: "It depends where you live."

Who can get general assistance?
In many states, such as New York and Pennsylvania, anyone who is not in a category, who cannot work or find a job, and who is needy can get general assistance. This includes families, couples, and single people.

Other states have peculiar requirements. For example, in Washington general assistance is provided to families of any age and single people over age fifty. Single people under fifty are completely out of luck.

In twenty-one states general assistance is available only to unemployable people, or to families without an employable member.[1] "Unemployable" means that the person is so mentally, physically, or emotionally disabled that he can't hold a job of any kind. In these twenty-one states it is *not* enough to show that you can't find a job. You must show that even if a job was available, you would not be strong enough to take it.

In the states and counties where general assistance is available to people who are able to work, the welfare officials will probably make you show that you have tried to find work but have been unsuccessful. In many places, people who apply for general assistance must report to the state employment office at least every two weeks to look for work. People who want general assistance must be willing to take nearly any sort of work offered to them. The work requirements for general assistance are more strict than the work rules for AFDC and they are also usually more strictly enforced.

How much money do general-assistance recipients receive?

Again, the answer varies from place to place. In some places people receive cash to meet any kind of basic need.[2] In other states, the individual normally receives no money, but only aid in kind or vouchers for groceries or rent. In some places welfare departments pay the same amount of money to people on general assistance as to

---

[1]
Arizona	Louisiana	North Carolina	Tennessee
D.C.	Maryland	North Dakota	Texas
Florida	Mississippi	Oklahoma	Virgin Islands
Georgia	Missouri	Puerto Rico	Virginia
Guam	New Mexico	South Carolina	West Virginia
Iowa			

HEW, SRS Characteristics of *General Assistance in the U.S.*, P.A. Rpt. #39, 1970

[2] States making money payments to eligible individuals and families for any kind of need include: Alaska, Arizona, Delaware, D.C., Hawaii, Maryland, Michigan, Minnesota, Missouri, New York, Pennsylvania, South Carolina, Utah.

those on ADC but in most places the general-assistance grant is smaller. In most states you can receive general assistance as long as your need continues. Some states limit the time you can receive general assistance. For example, in Alabama you can receive general assistance for only three months in any year and in Arkansas for only two months in any year.

Are there any rights to which all general-assistance recipients are entitled?

General-assistance recipients have no uniform substantive rights—that is, rights to specific items or amounts of money—but wherever they live they are entitled to equal treatment and fair procedures.

The states are not required to run any kind of general-assistance program at all, but once they do establish such a program it must follow these rules:

(1.) No one may be refused general assistance because he has not been in the state or county for some specified period of time as long as he is there now and intends to stay.[3]

(2.) No one may be refused general assistance because of his race or because he is not an American citizen.[4]

(3.) Everyone must be told the rules that govern general assistance, be allowed to apply for general assistance, be given a decision within reasonable time, and be given a chance to appeal and a fair hearing. Once a person starts receiving general assistance, his benefits may not be cut off until he has been given a notice of the reason for the proposed termination and the opportunity for a fair hearing.[5]

---

[3] *Shapiro v. Thompson,* 394 U.S. 618 (1969).
[4] *Graham v. Richardson,* 403 U.S. 365, (1971).
[5] *Goldberg v. Kelly,* 397 U.S. 254 (1970), *Alexander v. Silverman,* —— F.Supp. —— (E.D. Wisc. 1973), 2 CCH Pov. L. Rpt. ¶17,370, *Brooks v. Center Township,* —— F.2d. ——, (7th Cir. 1973), 2CCH Pov. L. Rpt. ¶17,588.

What can you do if your state provides inadequate general assistance?

The states are not legally required to provide general assistance so political organization, rather than a lawsuit, is required to make a state or local government increase the amount of aid it gives.

For example, in 1971 there was virtually no general assistance provided to poor people in Las Vegas, Nevada. If people did not fall into one of the federal categories, they could go to the county relief office to apply for food or medical relief. No money was ever provided. If people were hungry they would be given enough food for one day. If they could not pay their rent, they had to wait until they were thrown out on the street and they could then sleep in the city poorhouse. That was the full extent of general assistance in Las Vegas.

In 1971 the poor people in the city organized with the help of various welfare-rights organizations and went in large numbers to the county relief office to demand some changes. The protest demonstration met with phenomenal success. Not only does Las Vegas today have a general-assistance program, but it is probably the only one in the country that pays more than AFDC.

Do people receiving general assistance have any work rights?

Not many. The work regulations for people receiving general assistance are not very clear or helpful.

If you are receiving general assistance, your grant cannot be stopped for refusing work until you are given a chance for a hearing. Once you have begun receiving aid, you must be given clear notice of the reasons aid is being terminated and an opportunity for a fair hearing before aid actually stops. If you are expelled from a general-assistance work or training program, you must be given a written notice and a hearing, and aid must continue until after the hearing decision.[6]

Some work rules are so unfair and unequal that they may be illegal. For example, at one time the state of Georgia cut off welfare to black people during the cotton-chopping season. The state said that there was plenty of work for everyone, and that chopping cotton was suitable work for black mothers. A federal court said this plan was illegal because there might not be enough work for everyone, a particular mother might not be able to do field work and even if she worked she might not make enough to support her family, and that field work is no more "suitable" for black people than it is for white.[7] Unfortunately, a work program for general-assistance recipients must be outrageously unfair and unequal before it will be declared illegal.

---

[6]*Salandich v. Milwaukee County*, 351 F.Supp. 767 (E.D. Wisc. 1972).

[7]*Anderson v. Burson*, 300 F.Supp. 401 (N.D. Ga. 1968).

IV

Fair Hearings

When is a welfare recipient entitled to a fair hearing?
In most states welfare recipients may obtain a fair
hearing from the welfare department any time they have
a complaint or believe that they are being treated unfairly.
In every state, under the federal law you are legally entitled to a fair hearing any time that: (1) a request for
aid is denied; (2) a request for aid is not acted upon
within forty-five days; (3) a request for aid is only partly
granted; or (4) aid that you are receiving is reduced,
suspended, or terminated; (5) aid is paid in the form of
vendor or third party payments.[1]

What is a fair hearing?
A hearing is your chance to present your own arguments and facts. To do this well takes some preparation.
When the department sets the date of the hearing, they
must notify you enough in advance so that you have time
to prepare your case.[2] They must allow you, or your
friend or representative, to examine all the papers and
records which might be used at the hearing.[3] They must

[1] 45 C.F.R. §§205.10(a)(5) and (12).
[2] 45 C.F.R. §205.10(a)(8), welfare and Medicaid; 7 C.F.R.
§271.1(o)(3), food stamps.
[3] 45 C.F.R. §205.10(a)(13)(i), welfare and Medicaid; 7
C.F.R. §271.1(o)(3 and 4), food stamps.

72

keep records of previous fair-hearing decisions and must allow you to look at these.[4]

After requesting a fair hearing you should immediately get in contact with a welfare-rights organization or legal-services office to help you prepare. You may have only a short time to prepare, especially in reduction or termination cases where your benefits continue. There may be only five to ten days between the notices of the hearing and the hearing itself. During this time, you should obtain all facts on your side and also try to find out about the facts against you.

Are welfare recipients in every welfare program entitled to fair hearings?

Yes. Fair hearings must be given for complaints about your rights in any welfare program including the food-stamp program,[5] Medicaid, the Work Incentive Program, and cash benefits under the federal categorical programs or state general assistance.

How can a welfare recipient get a fair hearing?

In most states there is no special form or procedure for asking for a fair hearing. Any written or spoken demand for a "fair hearing" or appeal to a higher authority is acceptable. In 1973, federal regulations were amended to allow states to require that requests for fair hearings be in writing.[6] This rule may be unconstitutional. However, it is probably better to ask for a fair hearing in a letter and keep a copy so that the welfare department cannot say you didn't ask. The welfare department is not allowed to block your request for a fair hearing or discourage you from appealing. They should not tell you

[4] 45 C.F.R. §205.10(a)(19).
[5] 7 C.F.R. §271.1(n).
[6] 45 C.F.R. §205.10(a)(5)(i).

such things as "it won't do any good," and they can never
punish you for requesting a hearing or an appeal.[7]

Are you entitled to a hearing before the reduction or termination of aid?

Yes. Once you begin receiving welfare, Medicaid, or
food stamps you have a right to continue getting aid. If
the welfare department wants to reduce, suspend, or terminate your benefits, they must give you notice at least ten
days before the action is to be taken. The notice must be
in writing. It must tell you exactly why the Department
plans to cut your benefits. It must tell you that you have
a right to a hearing. It must tell you that, if you ask for
a hearing, the action will not be taken and your benefits
will not be cut until after the hearing has been held and
decided.[8] If the notice does not do all of these things,
it is an illegal notice. A new correct notice must be sent
before any action is taken against you, if you object to
the incorrect notice. No action can be taken until ten days
after the new notice.

Are there any circumstances in which your aid may be reduced or terminated without a prior hearing?

Yes. The right to a prior hearing does not apply where
the benefit is being cut as a result of a change in state
policy. If the state makes a new rule which applies to
everybody in similar circumstances, the welfare department must send you a notice telling you why your grant
is being reduced and what the new grant will be. But you
do not have a right to a hearing prior to the cut in

---

[7]45 C.F.R. §205.10(a)(5)(ii).
[8]45 C.F.R. §205.10(a)(4), Welfare and Medicaid. 7 C.F.R.
§271.1(n), food stamps. *Goldberg v. Kelly,* 397 U.S. 254
(1970).

benefits. If your benefit is cut because of a determination of fact or judgment about your particular case, you are entitled to a hearing prior to the termination or reduction of benefits.[9]

There are other exceptions to the rule that welfare recipients must be given a hearing prior to the termination of aid. For example, no prior notice or hearing need be offered where the department has information that the recipient has died, or where the recipient has stated, in writing, that he no longer wants aid.[10] The Nixon administration has proposed a regulation which would eliminate the right to a prior hearing in cases where the welfare department suspected fraud.[11]

When and where are welfare hearings held?

The hearings must be held at a date, time, and place that are reasonable.[12] If you are working, you should not need to miss work to have a hearing. If you are sick, or in a nursing home, the hearing should be held at your room. The hearing must be held as promptly as possible. The department must have the hearing, make a final decision and pay you within *ninety days* of the time of your request.[13]

What rights does a welfare recipient have at a fair hearing?

Fair hearings must meet the requirements of the United States Constitution for due process of law. Due process

---

[9] 45 C.F.R. §§205.10(a)(4)(iii) and (5).
[10] 45 C.F.R. §205.10(a)(4)(ii).
[11] 38 Fed. Reg. 22006 (Aug. 15, 1973).
[12] 45 C.F.R. §205.10(a)(8).
[13] 45 C.F.R. §205.10(a)(16); *Jeffries v. Swank,* 337 F.Supp. 1062 (N.D. Ill. 1971); *King v. Martin,* 21 Cal. App. 3rd 791 (1971).

means "fundamental fairness." Federal law specifically provides that:

(1.) The hearing official must be a person who was not involved in the original decision about your case.

(2.) If your case concerns a medical question, the medical official must be someone who was not involved in the original decision and must be someone whom you and the welfare department accept.

(3.) You can present your own case or have a lawyer or any other person of your choice present your case for you.

(4.) You can bring witnesses to speak in your behalf.

(5.) You can cross-examine any witnesses whom the welfare department uses.

(6.) You can present arguments or evidence to refute evidence against you.

(7.) You can present your case in a convenient and informal way.

(8.) The decision must be based solely on the spoken and written evidence presented at the hearing.

(9.) You have a right to a final decision and action on your hearing within ninety days from the date you requested it.

(10.) You must be notified in writing of the decision. This notice must state the specific reasons for the decision and give the evidence that supports it.

Does winning a fair hearing guarantee the right to back payments and benefits?

Yes. If you win your fair hearing, you have a legal right to back payments and benefits from the time that the incorrect action was first taken.[14] For example, suppose that a family is receiving AFDC. In January their cousin, who is also a needy child, comes to live with them and the mother informs the caseworker. In March

---

[14] 45 C.F.R. §205.10(a)(18), and 206.10(a)(6).

the grant still has not been increased to take care of the cousin's needs, so the mother requests a fair hearing. In May the hearing is held and in July there is a fair-hearing decision favorable to the family. The family is entitled to back payments from January to July. Such a slow hearing process is illegal, but not unusual. The slowness of the process makes the payment of back benefits very important.

What is a group hearing?

Sometimes many people have the same complaint against the welfare department. For example, a refusal by the department to give special grants to buy children clothing for school affects everybody who has school-age children and not enough money to buy them clothing. In this situation it is sometimes best to organize a campaign and get as many people as possible to ask for fair hearings. When many people ask for hearings in which the only issue is the same department policy, everyone can come to one big hearing.[15] A hearing in which many people bring the same complaint against the department may be more effective than one person complaining alone.

Until 1973 the individual had a right to decide whether he or she wanted a group or individual hearing. Under the new Nixon regulations, individuals do not have a right to a group hearing unless the welfare department wants to do it that way. On the other hand, the welfare department can force you to appeal your case in group hearing, even if you would rather have an individual hearing, if the sole issue is one of State or Federal law or policy or changes in State or Federal law. However, even in a group hearing you must be allowed to present your own case and be represented by your own representative.[16]

---

[15] 45 C.F.R. §205.10(a)(5)(iv).
[16] 45 C.F.R. §205.10(a)(5)(iv).

Can a welfare recipient withdraw a request for a fair hearing?

Yes. After you ask for a fair hearing the caseworker may talk to you about your complaint to try to settle it without going to a hearing. But if the department will not give you everything that you believe is your right, you do not need to settle the case. Only you can decide to withdraw your request for a fair hearing.

If you are not able to go to the fair hearing when it is scheduled, you should let the welfare department know as soon as possible. Until 1973, the rule was that if you did not appear at the hearing the welfare department was supposed to try to contact you before ruling that you had abandoned your request for a hearing.[17] Now the welfare department can deem your case abandoned if you fail to appear without good cause.[18]

What can you do when a fair hearing isn't useful or fair?

When you apply for welfare and the welfare department takes more than forty-five days to act on your application, you can have a fair hearing. But a hearing is not very useful if what you need is money for food and rent. More and more welfare departments are effectively denying aid to people simply by failing to act on applications and making it difficult for people to apply for aid. A court in California found that over one half of the applications for Aid to the Disabled were not acted upon within sixty days as required by law.[19] A court in Connecticut found that over one half of the applications for

---

[17]Fed. Handbook of Public Assistance Admin. §6300(f).
[18]45 C.F.R. §205.10(a)(5)(v).
[19]*Committee for the Rights of the Disabled v. Carleson*, 2 CCH Pov. L. Rpt. ¶15,542 (Calif. Super. Ct. 1971).

ADC were not acted on within thirty days as required by law.[20] Welfare departments are also illegally slow in rendering fair-hearing decisions.

When the welfare department breaks the law more often than it obeys it, it is very difficult to take action on an individual basis, but it may be useful to get together with other welfare recipients and go to the welfare centers to insist that the law be obeyed. Or get in contact with a lawyer. In these situations courts have ordered welfare officials to comply with time limits for action on applications or fair-hearing decisions, ordered retroactive benefits for recipients whose applications were illegally delayed,[21] ordered welfare officials to pay a fine of one hundred dollars to recipients injured by departmental delay,[22] set up a system for federal court supervision of the administration of fair hearings,[23] and ordered that applicants be presumed eligible and given aid thirty days after their application.[24]

---

[20]*Class v. White* —— F.Supp. —— (D. Conn. 1972), 2 CCH Pov. L. Rpt. ¶16,314.

[21]*Alvarado v. Houston*, —— F.Supp. —— (W.D. Mich. 1971).

[22]*Rodriguez v. Swank*, 318 F.Supp. 289 (N.D. Ill. 1970), aff'd 403 U.S. 901 (1971), *sub nom Rodriguez v. Weaver* —— F.Supp. —— (1972) (contempt proceeding). 2 CCH Pov. L. Rpt. ¶16,357.

[23]*Alemnares v. Wyman*, 334 F.Supp. 512 (S.D.N.Y. 1971), aff'd 453 F.2d 1075 (2nd Cir. 1971), *cert. denied* 405 U.S. 944 (1972).

[24]*Alvarado v. Houston*, ——F.Supp. —— (W.D. Mich. 1971) *Gonzalez v. Westcott*, Super. Ct. of N.J. Law Div., Hudson Co. Docket No. 39068-69 P.W.

V

Health Services

A. Medicaid

What is Medicaid?

The Medicaid Program was created by the federal government in 1965 to give health care and services to people who cannot afford them. It is paid for by the federal, state, and local government. *Medicaid* is not the same as *Medicare*. *Medicare*, which is described on pages 92–101 is for anybody, rich or poor, who is sixty-five or older. *Medicaid* is for poor people only. If you are both poor and old you may be able to get both Medicare and Medicaid. Medicaid will pay for the medical expenses that Medicare does not and also will cover Medicare expenses such as the monthly premium and the deductible.

Medicaid is not charity. It is a right like the right of children to attend public school to which you are entitled by law. Medicaid is paid for by taxes and everybody pays taxes, including poor people. The doctors at the hospital you go to with a Medicaid card are not giving you charity. They will be paid by the department of welfare.

Who can get Medicaid?

A state can decide to give Medicaid to everyone. However, the federal government will pay most of the cost of Medicaid for people in the following groups. The federal government pays between 50 percent and 83 percent of the costs of Medicaid, depending on how wealthy the state is. The state pays the rest.

(1.) *Everybody who gets categorical welfare assistance.* You automatically get Medicaid if you receive money from welfare for:

(a.) aid to dependent children;

(b.) aid to the aged;

(c.) aid to the permanently and totally disabled;

(d.) aid to the blind.

The forms you fill out to apply for welfare automatically get you a Medicaid card. This Medicaid card will allow everyone in your family who gets money from welfare also to get health care from Medicaid. Every state, except Arizona and Alaska, now has an approved Medicaid program for these people.

(2.) *Everybody who is eligible for categorical aid but not getting it.* It is hard to understand why anyone would be entitled to categorical money payments and not get them. But if someone does not want to take welfare for some reason, he can still get Medicaid separately.[1]

(3.) *ADC children under twenty-one.* All children under twenty-one must be given Medicaid if their families qualify for ADC on the basis of need and deprivation of parental support. States may not deny Medicaid to a person under twenty-one on grounds that he is not attending school, or not attending the right kind of school. Under this rule only the child gets Medicaid; his parents do not.[2]

(4.) *Other needy children under twenty-one.* The states *may* give Medicaid to all needy children under twenty-one even though they are not eligible for financial assistance under ADC or any other category. They do not need to live with their parents to be eligible. They can be children

---

[1] 45 C.F.R. §248.10(b)(2)(i).

[2] 42 U.S.C. §1396a(b)2.

who have two parents in the home. They can be children whose parents are working but do not earn enough to pay their children's medical-care expenses. The states listed with a Number 1 on the chart at the back of the book pay Medicaid to all needy children under the age of twenty-one.

(5.) *The medically needy*. These are people whose income and resources are large enough to cover their daily living expenses—according to the welfare's definition of need—but do not have enough to pay for medical care. The medically needy can earn one-third as much as the amount paid for ADC to a family. The "medically needy" must also be aged, disabled, blind, or members of families with dependent children.[3]

Not every state gives Medicaid to the medically needy. The states that do give Medicaid to the medically needy are listed with a number II, on the chart at the back of the book. The chart also tells the income levels for the medically needy. If a state decides to give Medicaid to the medically needy people in one category—for example, blind people—they must give it to the medically needy in all categories.[4]

What does the right to "spend down" to Medicaid mean?

If a state provides Medicaid for the medically needy, it must allow people to "spend down" to eligibility levels. This means that if your income is above the limit for the medically needy, but you spend all of the excess income on medical bills, then you can get the rest of your medical expenses paid for by Medicaid.

For example, in Hawaii the medical need level for a family of four is $3600 a year. Suppose that a family in Hawaii earns $5,000 a year. They have a very sick child

---

[3] 42 U.S.C. §1396a(a)(10).
[4] 45 C.F.R. §248.10(b)(3).

who spends several weeks in the hospital. The hospital bill is $1,500.

$$
\begin{array}{rl}
& \text{Income} \quad = \$5,000 \\
\text{minus} & \underline{\text{Medical bills} = 1,500} \\
& \$3,500 = \text{Money for living}
\end{array}
$$

After paying the hospital bill, this family will be eligible for Medicaid for the whole family, for the whole next year.

You can count almost any kind of medical bill to spend down to medical-assistance levels. You can count any bills for health insurance and any medical services "recognized under state law."[5] You can count bills for anything which would be paid for by Medicaid, plus other things that Medicaid does not usually provide such as dentures, plastic surgery, orthodonture, contact lenses, eyeglasses, and psychiatric care. Bills for any of these things should be counted in spending down to medically needy levels.

Unfortunately, people who live in states that don't have a program for the medically needy cannot spend down. This means that in a state like Colorado, which has no program for the medically needy, a person who has income just a little over public-assistance levels will not be able to get Medicaid no matter how much he spends on medical bills. So far the courts have said that it is legal for the states that do not have a program for the medically needy not to allow spending down.[6]

(6.) *Persons in medical facilities.* In some states, (See chart number III), Medicaid is paid to anyone who would be eligible for assistance payments if he were not a patient in a medical facility. (One exception to this rule is the person under sixty-five who is a patient in a mental or tuberculosis hospital.) This includes people in medical

---

[5]45 C.F.R. §248.21(a)(3)(ii)(b).

[6]See *Fullington v. Shea*, 320 F.Supp. 500 (D. Colo. 1970), *aff'd*, 404 U.S. 963 (1971).

facilities who have enough money to meet their personal needs outside the facility under the state need levels.[7]

(7.) *Close relatives caring for children under the age of twenty-one.* These people can get Medicaid in some states if they are needy. The relatives must be those who are close enough to make an ADC family. See pages 21–29. States which pay Medicaid to close relatives are listed on the chart with number IV.

(8.) *People over twenty-one who actually receive general assistance.* In a few states, everyone who gets general assistance can also get Medicaid. The states that give Medicaid to these people are listed with a number V on the chart.

(9.) *Medically needy people, not in any category.* Some states give Medicaid to people who are not in any category, and are not receiving public assistance, but who have income just over public-assistance levels. These states are listed on the chart with a number VI. The income-eligibility levels for these people are the same as for the medically needy and are listed on the chart.

May a person's relatives be legally required to pay for his medical care?

A person or family's eligibility for Medicaid is determined only by the income and resources they actually have. Just as in public assistance, support from relatives living away from home can only be counted if it is *actually* available to meet *current* needs on a regular basis.[8] There are fewer legally responsible relatives under Medicaid than under public assistance. Spouses are liable for the support of each other and parents are liable for the support of their children who are under twenty-one, blind, or disabled. In determining Medicaid eligibility the states cannot make

---

[7]Handbook of Public Assistance Administration, Supp. D., §4040.2 and 4050 B.

[8]45 C.F.R. §248.21(a)(2)(i).

children responsible for their parents or any other relatives responsible for each other.[9]

Is there a duty to repay medicaid?

No. Unlike public assistance, there is absolutely *no obligation to repay* any benefits received under Medicaid if they were correctly paid at the time. If you get a good job or win a million dollars in the lottery, you will no longer be eligible for Medicaid but you cannot be required to repay any benefits you have already received.[10]

Does Medicaid pay the full bill?

No. Until 1973 Medicaid paid the full bill for services covered and doctors and hospitals were prohibited from making extra charges to people eligible for Medicaid. Now Congress has amended the law to say that the aged, blind, disabled, and the medically needy must pay a premium to obtain Medicaid coverage. The premium must be related to the individual's income. In addition the states are now allowed to require all people eligible for Medicaid to make a co-payment for services that they receive. Co-payments must be nominal in amount.[11]

What will Medicaid pay for?

Medicaid will pay for a great many, but not all, medical expenses. This section will tell you many of the things paid for by Medicaid but it does not include everything. Don't assume that because something is not mentioned here that it is not covered. Also, as with all welfare programs, Medicaid payments vary from state to state.

---

[9] 42 U.S.C. §1396a(a)(17)(D), 45 C.F.R. §248.21(a)(2)(ii).
[10] 42 U.S.C. 1396a(a)(18).
[11] 42 U.S.C. §§1396a(a)(14),(15).

You should also know that Medicaid will only pay your outstanding bills. It will not reimburse you for cash that you have laid out. Therefore, always try to be billed and avoid paying cash for services if you think that you can get Medicaid to pay for the services.

INPATIENT HOSPITAL CARE

If you go to the hospital, Medicaid will pay the cost of a semi-private room (fewer than six people) and all doctors' fees, laboratory tests, and x-rays while you are in the hospital. Hospitals do not give charity to Medicaid patients. On the contrary, they normally get as much money from Medicaid as they get from Blue Cross for care given to the people it insures. If you are placed on a ward, or given second-class treatment of any sort, you are being cheated by the hospital. The hospital is paid to give you the best treatment.

How much does Medicaid pay for hospital care?

Medicaid will pay the whole hospital bill. Some hospitals try to collect deposits, or extra charges from Medicaid patients. You should refuse to pay any such fees. Medicaid will pay whatever the hospital decides is reasonable for the care it has given you.[12] Hospitals and doctors who participate in Medicaid must agree to accept the Medicaid payments in full payment of their bills. It is illegal for the hospital or the doctor to try to collect additional money from the public-assistance patient.[13]

[12]45 C.F.R. 250.30(b)(1). *Catholic Hospital v. Rockefeller*, 305 F.Supp. 1256 (E.D.N.Y. 1969), remanded, 397 U.S. 820 (1970); *new decree*, 430 F.2d 1297 (2nd Cir. 1970).

[13]45 C.F.R. §250.30(a)(6), *Society of Hospitals v. Mogenson*, 165 N.Y.L.J. #4, p. 18, 65 Misc. 2d 278 (N.Y. Civ. Ct. 1971), and *Knickerbocker Hospital v. Downing, 165 N.Y.L.J. #41, p. 20 (N.Y. Civ. Ct. 1971)*.

What hospital care does Medicaid pay for?

The states and hospitals may not eliminate certain groups of patients or certain diagnoses from Medicaid coverage. (Except tuberculosis and mental illness, which are not covered by Medicaid.) Thus every state must include in-patient hospital services for any sort of care that is medically necessary and reasonable. A state cannot refuse to make Medicaid payments for hospitalization needed in connection with an abortion.[14] A state may limit the number of days of hospitalization that it pays for under Medicaid, provided that the services provided are "sufficient in amount, duration, and scope reasonably to achieve their purpose."[15] Token services are not enough.[16] These words are vague and they mean different things in different states.

What hospitals can Medicaid patients go to?

Freedom of choice is guaranteed under Medicaid.[17] You can go to any hospital that agrees to serve you. The hospital must be qualified to participate in the Medicaid program, but all good ones are. You do not need to go to a hospital simply because you live close to it. You do not need to go to a general, city, or county hospital. Poor people can now go to the private hospital of their choice and Medicaid will pay for their care. Many people are in the habit of going to the public hospital, and continue to go there even though it may not be as good or convenient for them. If you need treatment requiring special equip-

---

[14]*Klein v. Nassau Co. Medical Center*, 347 F.Supp. 496 (E.D.N.Y. 1972), *remanded*, 412 U.S. 925 (1973).

[15]45 C.F.R. §249.10(a)(5).

[16]HEW Handbook of Public Asst. Administration Supp. D., §5140.

[17]45 C.F.R. §249.11; 42 U.S.C. §1396a(a)(23).

ment or skill, find out where you can get it and go there.
Find out where you can get the best treatment. If they will
take you, Medicaid will pay for it and you have a right to
it.

OUTPATIENT CARE

Medicaid in every state must also pay for outpatient
hospital care, which is "sufficient in amount, duration, and
scope reasonably to achieve its purposes."[18] It must also
pay for the laboratory and x-ray services needed either
in the hospital or on an outpatient basis.[19] Medicaid must
pay for a physician's services whether rendered in his office,
the patient's home, the hospital, a nursing home, or else-
where.[20]

**Are there any limits on outpatient care that Medicaid will
pay for?**

Yes. Every state must provide the basic outpatient services listed above. Unfortunately, the states are free to
limit the amount of service—for example, the number
of doctor visits—that they will pay for under Medicaid. The
states are also free to require prior authorization for services. However, the Medicaid program must be run so that
eligibility can be determined and medical care and services
be provided in a manner "consistent with simplicity of administration and the best interests of the individual" and
without cumbersome procedures.[21] Again, these are vague
words, but if getting services is so complicated that it is
practically impossible for a person—especially a person
who is sick—to get them, then the state program is probably illegal.

[18] 45 C.F.R. §249.10(a)(5).
[19] 42 U.S.C. §1396d(a)3.
[20] U.S.C. §1396d(a)5.
[21] 42 U.S.C. §1396a(a)19.

Although Medicaid must pay hospitals their full "reasonable costs," in many places Medicaid does not pay doctors who work outside of hospitals as much as they can get from people who have money. Medicaid is supposed to pay as much for poor people as people with money normally pay.[22] This is an important issue for people to organize and fight around because if doctors are being paid too little they will not give good service.

NURSING HOMES

Every state must provide Medicaid money for skilled nursing-home services for needy people twenty-one years of age or older.[23] States participating in Medicaid are required to have licensing standards for nursing homes and nursing-home administrators which require high-quality care.[24] Unfortunately, in most states these standards are not enforced and political organization is required to make state-licensing agencies enforce their standards.

What rights do nursing-home patients have?

Under Medicaid, nursing-home patients are allowed to keep some money every month for their personal needs—extra food, magazines, cigarettes, clothing. Nursing-home patients also have all of the rights that every other United States citizen has. They can meet together, receive visitors, and express their opinions without fear of punishment. Again, these rights are frequently not granted and lawsuits and political pressure may be necessary.

----

[22]45 C.F.R. §250.30(a)(5), amended 36 Fed. Reg. 21591, Nov. 11, 1971, Also, Handbook of Public Assistance Administration, Supp.D., §5330.

[23]42 U.S.C. §1396d(a)4.

[24]45 C.F.R. §249.33 and §252.10.

SERVICES FOR CHILDREN UNDER TWENTY-ONE

Every state must organize a program to provide early
and periodic screening, diagnosis and treatment for all children under twenty-one (EPSDT).[25] To get most Medicaid
services, the recipient must find a doctor or hospital willing
to provide treatment, and then Medicaid will pay the bill.
In many areas of the country poor people cannot find doctors or the doctors do not like to treat poor people or
deal with Medicaid. EPSDT is different. The state *must*
organize a program to make sure that children received
early and periodic screening, diagnosis, and treatment.[26]
The welfare department must tell the community about
EPSDT. For example, they should sponsor mass-media ad-
vertising about the importance of regular health care and
tell people where to get screening and treatment services.
Welfare workers must also be hired to go into poor communities to inform families about how to get regular medical care. The program must provide transportation and
child-care services to assure that children will receive
regular screening and treatment. The EPSDT program must
be organized to make sure that children receive treatment
for all physical and mental defects which are found in the
screening. Treatment must include dental care, eye glasses,
and hearing aids, as well as all of the other services
available under the state's Medicaid program.

Even though the federal law requiring the states to set
up an EPSDT program has been on the books since 1969,
as of 1972 not one state had a program which met all of
the federal requirements. States will not organize an effective EPSDT program unless poor people demand that a
program be organized for their children. Headstart Parents,

---

[25] 42 U.S.C. §1396d(4)(B).
[26] 45 C.F.R. §249.10(a)(3)(iv). Federal Guidelines M.S.A.,
June 28, 1972.

welfare-rights organizations, and other poor people's groups should insist that the state organize this program, and offer suggestions on how the program can be organized to meet people's needs for adequate health-care services.

FAMILY PLANNING SERVICES

Every state which participates in Medicaid or Aid to Familes with Dependent Children must establish a program to provide family planning services and supplies to individuals of childbearing age who desire such services and supplies.[27] Services must also be available to young people who are sexually active. Every person who receives Medicaid or ADC must be told of the availability of family planning services and offered help in arranging to get the services which they want. Federal law also requires that services be offered on a voluntary basis. A woman cannot be forced to accept services which she does not want.

TRANSPORTATION NECESSARY TO OBTAIN MEDICAL SERVICES

Every state must provide some method of transportation to and from hospitals, clinics, and doctors for people on Medicaid.[28] The state may provide ambulance service, or money to allow people to use public transportation, or some other method.

---

[27] 42 U.S.C. §602(a)(14) and (15) and 606(d) (ADC). 42 U.S.C. §1396d(a)(4)(C). (Medicaid). 45 C.F.R. §220.21.
[28] 45 C.F.R. 249.10(a)(5).

OTHER SERVICES

Every state must provide the services described on pages 86–91. In addition states can, and some do, provide a wide range of other services including dental services, home-health care, private-duty nursing, clinic services, physical therapy, drugs, dentures, prosthetic devices, prescription eye glasses.

What procedural rights do people have under Medicaid?

People applying for Medicaid have all the same rights as people applying for public assistance. If you have a complaint about Medicaid, you have the fair-hearing rights described on pages 72–79. Once you begin receiving Medicaid you must receive a fair hearing before your benefits can be cut off or reduced.

B. Medicare

Who is entitled to Medicare?

Everyone who is sixty-five or older and eligible for Social Security or railroad-retirement benefits gets Medicare.[29] Also people over the age of eighteen who have been eligible for social-security disability benefits for twenty-four months may receive Medicare. You do not need to be poor to get Medicare.

When you reach sixty-five you should get a Medicare card from the social security office. When a husband and wife both have Medicare, they receive separate cards and claim numbers.

---

[29] 42 U.S.C. §1395c.

Medicare has two parts: (1) Part A, Hospital Insurance, which everybody gets automatically; (2) Part B, Medical and Doctors Insurance, is optional, and you get it only if you sign up and pay for it.

What are the basic Part A benefits?

When a Medicare recipient gets sick and needs to go to the hospital, in each "benefit period" Medicare will *help* pay for inpatient hospital services for up to ninety days, *and* post-hospital skilled nursing-home care for up to one hundred days, *and* home health-care services.[30]

What is a benefit period?

A benefit period is simply a period of time during which you use hospital insurance benefits. The first time you enter a hospital after you reach sixty-five will be the beginning of your first benefit period. You first benefit period ends as soon as you have *not* been a bed patient in any hospital or skilled nursing home for sixty days in a row. After that, a new benefit period begins the next time you enter a hospital and that benefit period ends as soon as another sixty days in a row have passed during which you have not been a bed patient in any hospital. Then another benefit period can begin the next time you enter a hospital—and so on. There is no limit to the number of benefit periods you may have. For each new benefit period, your full hospital insurance benefits are available again to use as you need them.[31]

What hospital services will Medicare pay for?

In order to receive hospital insurance, you must be ad-

[30]42 U.S.C. §1395d.
[31]U.S.C. 1395d.

mitted to the hospital by a doctor, who must certify that
you need to be cared for in the hospital. You and your
doctor can choose the hospital you go to, but, except in
an emergency situation, it must be a hospital which has
joined the Medicare program. All the good hospitals have
joined Medicare, but you should make sure in advance.
While you are in the hospital Medicare will pay for: semi-
private room and all meals, nursing, drugs, tests, x-rays,
medical supplies, and medical social services. Medicare
will *not* pay for TV, radio, or telephone, a private-duty
nurse, or a private room or *doctor's services*. (To get doctor bills paid you must enroll in Part B.)

How much will Medicare pay for?

You must pay the first seventy-two dollars of the hospital
bill in each "benefit period." In addition, you must pay
eighteen dollars a day, from the sixty-first to the ninetieth
day you are in the hospital.[32] Medicare pays the hospital
directly. You do not see the bill. Medicare will send you
a statement when they have paid the bill.

May a hospital require an advance deposit?

Many hospitals require that Medicare patients pay a
deposit before they are admitted. *This is illegal.* Hospitals
cannot require, as a condition of admission, that you pay a
deposit.[33]

---

[32]The deductible and co-insurance is less if the spell of illness
began before 1973.

[33]"A provider of services may not deny covered inpatient
services to an individual entitled to have payment made for
such services on the ground of his inability or failure to pay
a requested amount on or before admission." 20 C.F.R. 405.10.

What happens if you need more than ninety days hospitalization?

Every Medicare patient has a lifetime reserve of sixty additional hospital days. You can use these extra days if you ever need more than ninety days of hospital care in the same benefit period. For each lifetime reserve day used you must pay thirty-six dollars a day, and Medicare pays the rest.

What nursing-home care will Part A cover?

Nursing-home benefits under Medicare are very limited.

To get nursing-home services paid for by Medicare you must: (1) have the doctor certify that you need skilled nursing care; (2) have been in the hospital for at least three days in a row before going to the nursing home; (3) enter the nursing home within fourteen days after you leave the hospital (or within twenty-eight days if there is no nursing-home bed available before then, or within a longer period if the illness is one that requires active treatment only after a period of convalescence (e.g., hip fractures); (4) enter the nursing home for the same condition that was treated in the hospital; and (5) go to a skilled nursing home that has joined the Medicare program.

If you meet all of these requirements Medicare must help pay for a bed in a semi-private room, meals, regular nursing services, drugs, medical supplies, physical, occupational and speech therapy, and medical social services. It will not pay for doctors services, TV, radio, telephones, private rooms, or private-duty nurses. You must pay a co-insurance of nine dollars per day for each day after the twentieth day of skilled nursing-home care.[84]

---

[84]The co-insurance is less for spells of illness beginning before 1973.

If you leave a skilled nursing home and are then re-admitted within fourteen days, you can continue to use your additional days for that benefit period without a new three-day stay in the hospital.

What home health benefits does Part A provide?

After you have been in the hospital or in a skilled nursing home covered by Medicare, you are entitled to a maximum of one hundred home health visits for up to a year after discharge from the hospital or nursing home if: (1) you were in a hospital for at least three days in a row; (2) you are confined to your home; (3) the doctor decides, within fourteen days after your discharge from the hospital or nursing home, that you need nursing care or speech or physical therapy; and (4) the home health care is for the same condition that you were treated for in the hospital.

How do you sign up for Part B?

Part B of Medicare is an insurance program that pays for inpatient doctors' services and some outpatient services. It is an optional program that people pay to join. The government wants to encourage people to sign up for Part B Medicare. If you get Social Security checks, the monthly premium will be deducted automatically after you sign up. If you do not receive Social Security, you will need to make monthly payments to your Social Security office. You can sign up for Medicare Part B during a general enrollment period which takes place each year from January 1 to March 31.

You can stop your Medicare Part B insurance any time. If you do cancel your medical insurance, you have only one chance to get it back. You may sign up in any general enrollment period within three years after you cancel.

What does it cost?

The Medicare Part B enrollment fee varies between $3.00 and $8.70 a month, depending upon when you turned sixty-five and when you enrolled in Medicare. The enrollment fee is lowest if you enroll at age sixty-five. It goes up ten percent each year after that.

What does Part B help pay for?

Doctors. It will help pay for medical or surgical services provided by a doctor of medicine or osteopathy, services of podiatrists, dental surgery, and other services ordinarily furnished in a doctor's office, such as tests, supplies, and drugs which you cannot give to yourself. You can go to any doctor. Part B will not pay for ordinary dentist services, routine physical checkups, routine food care, treatment of flat feet, eye examinations, hearing examinations, immunizations, Christian Science practitioners, Chiropractors, or Naturopathes.

Ambulance. Part B will help pay for ambulance services when the ambulance meets Medicare requirements, when it would be dangerous to move the patient in any other way, and when the patient is taken to a facility in his locality.

Outpatient Hospital Services. Part B will *help* pay for services that you get at an outpatient clinic of a hospital which is in the Medicare program. Services that are covered include: laboratory tests, x-rays, emergency-room services, and medical supplies such as splints and casts. Medicare will not pay for routine physicals, eye exams, hearing exams, or immunizations.

Home Health Benefits. Part B will help pay for a visiting, part-time nurse, physical or speech therapist if your doctors say you need it and you are confined to your own home.

It will *not* pay for housekeepers or health aides, for drugs, or for full-time nursing care.

Does Medicare Part B pay the entire cost of Medicare care?

No.Medical insurance does not pay any of the first fifty dollars in each calendar year of the reasonable charges for covered services. Reasonable charges are determined by Blue Shield or a similar organization in your area. After Medicare records show that your bills for a year are over fifty dollars, Medicare will pay *80 percent* of the reasonable charges for covered services for the rest of that year. You must pay the other 20 percent. Be sure to save your bills so that you can show when you have spent fifty dollars for covered services.

There is only *one* fifty-dollar medical insurance deductible for each year—not a separate fifty-dollar deductible for each kind of covered service. Also, if you paid medical bills yourself for covered services in October, November or December, those bills can count toward your fifty-dollar deductible in the next year.

Will Medicare Part B pay for inpatient doctors' services for x-rays and lab tests?

Yes. Medicare Part B will pay all—100 percent—of the reasonable charges by doctors for radiology services and pathology services which you receive as an inpatient in a qualified Medicare hospital.

How is the money paid under Part B?

Insurance payments under Part B can be made directly to you or they may be made directly to your doctor, if you both agree. If you and your doctor agree that he will apply for the Medicare benefits, you will both fill out a form and send it to Social Security. He will be paid directly and will send you a bill for the 20 percent of his reasonable charges, which you must pay.

If either you or the doctor do not want to have Social Security pay him directly, the payment will be made to you. You can make a claim whether or not you have paid the bill. The doctor will fill out a form or give you an itemized bill. You complete and sign Part 1 of the Request for Medicare Payment form. (These are normally available at the doctor's office and someone there can help to fill it out.) You send the bill and the form to Blue Shield or the other organization that handles Medicare in your area. (A list of those organizations can be obtained from Social Security.) You should send the bill and claim in as soon as possible.

Will Medicaid pay Medicare costs for poor people?

In most states, the Medicaid program will pay the Part B premium for all older people who are eligible for Medicaid. These states are listed with a number VII in the chart. Medicaid in these states will also pay the Medicare deposit and the co-insurance under Part A for people who are both old and poor.

What is the difference between medical and custodial care?

Because of the high cost of the Medicare program, Medicare has announced that it will pay only for medical services and not what they call "custodial services." Often it is not easy to know which is which. For example, if a doctor prescribes rest in a nursing home for a patient, Medicare may very well decide that the patient was not receiving medical care but rather was just being provided with room and board, and therefore will refuse to pay the bills. In the past, Medicare has often refused to pay bills in these cases.

In 1972 Congress tried to solve this problem by a law which says if the patient believed, in good faith, that the care he received was medically necessary the patient cannot be forced to pay the bill.[85] If Medicare refuses to pay and the hospital or nursing home sues the patient, the Medicare program will pay the bill for the patient and then deduct money from future payments to that hospital or nursing home. If your doctor has prescribed hospital or nursing-home services, and you believe that you needed those services, you should not have to pay the bill even if the Medicare program later decides that the service was not medically necessary.

Where can you get more information on Medicare?

As you can see, Medicare is very complicated. The information given here is just the very basic facts. You can get booklets and answers to some questions at your local Social Security Office or from the U.S. Printing Office, Washington, D.C. 20402.

Can a hospital or doctor refuse to serve Medicaid and Medicare patients?

Private doctors and profit-making hospitals can refuse to take Medicaid and Medicare. No private doctor is required to accept any patient and many doctors in fact refuse to care for people whose bills are paid for by Medicaid or Medicare. Some think that the payment is too low. Others dislike the red tape. Some may simply be prejudiced against minority-group members, a disproportionate number of whom are poor and in need of free medical services. The willingness of doctors to accept these patients varies from

---

[85]42 U.S.C. §1395pp. Soc. Sec. Act §1879, as amended, P.L. 92-603, 1972.

place to place. Private clinics and profit-making hospitals can also refuse to serve Medicaid or Medicare recipients.

Nonprofit hospitals must accept Medicaid and Medicare. Most hospitals are nonprofit. Those run by churches, religious orders, or universities almost certainly are. Nonprofit hospitals do not pay state or federal taxes. These hospitals are prohibited by federal law from discrimination on the basis of source of payment.[36]

What health services are available to poor people who don't have Medicaid or Medicare?

Many millions of people in America are not poor enough for Medicaid, or old enough for Medicare, but simply do not have the money to buy the health care that they need. In fact, you can make a very good wage and still not have enough money to buy decent health care. Hospitals in many places cost one hundred dollars a day or more just for the room and board—and a lot more for tests, doctors, x-rays, and so forth. An operation or a serious illness is a disaster for people who have no insurance or insufficient insurance.

For routine hospital care, a person who is poor, but not poor enough for Medicaid, can go to a public hospital or to a private hospital which has received Hill-Burton funds. Your right to hospital care in an emergency is somewhat broader and will be discussed separately.

Public Hospitals

These hospitals and their clinics often make adjustments in fees on the basis of ability to pay, or give free care to poor people who do not qualify for Medicaid. However, the public hospitals are often overcrowded and it may be difficult to get in even if you cannot afford to go anyplace else.

---

[36]IRS Rev. Ruling 69-545, 1969 Comm. Bill.

Hill-Burton Hospitals

The Hill-Burton Act is a federal law which gives non-profit hospitals money for construction. In exchange, the hospitals promise to "provide a reasonable volume of services to persons unable to pay therefor."[37] Over one third of the hospital beds in the United States were built with this federal money. The government has not made the hospitals keep their promises. In several states, courts have said that the private hospitals which got the Hill-Burton money must provide care to people who are not able to pay.[38]

Hill-Burton hospitals must provide free care to people who cannot pay which is worth 10 percent of all grants received, or 3 percent of their annual operating costs.[39] Or a hospital may comply by certifying that it never turns people away because of their inability to pay. Hospitals are supposed to submit annual compliance reports to the state Hill-Burton agency (which is usually the department of welfare). Many Hill-Burton hospitals do not obey these requirements. People who need hospitals services should investigate the situation in their area before they get sick and insist that hospitals begin providing free care.

Emergency Services

Even if you are acutely ill or injured you may have trouble getting treatment in the emergency rooms of some hospitals. This is what the law requires in cases of acute emergency:

(1.) In every state, if a hospital begins to give you treat-

---

[37] 42 U.S.C. §291c(e).

[38] *Cook v. Ochsner Foundation Hospital*, 319 F.Supp. 603, (E.D. La. 1970); *Organized Migrants in Community Action v. Jones Archer Smith Hospital*, 325 F.Supp. 268 (S.D. Fla. 1971); *Perry v. The Greater Southwest Community Hospital Foundation, Inc.*, —— F.Supp. —— (D.C.D.C. 1971). *Euresti v. Stenner*, 458 F.2d 1115 (10th Cir. 1972), rehearing den., June 13, 1972.

[39] 42 C.F.R. §53.111(d)(i).

ment, they must continue to treat you until the emergency has passed.

(2.) In Illinois, California, and North Carolina the legislature has required that every hospital provide emergency care to people who need it.[40]

(3.) In Delaware and Missouri the courts have held that any hospital that has an emergency room must provide care to people, whether or not they can pay, in cases of real emergency.[41] In other states, the courts have not recently been asked to decide whether a hospital must treat true emergency cases. If a hospital refuses emergency care, you may be able to sue and collect money if the patient is further injured or dies. But that is not much help when what you wanted was treatment.

What other health services are available to poor people?

Neighborhood Health and Mental Health Centers provide special services to poor people. These centers are located in neighborhoods where poor people live. They are financed by the U.S. Office of Economic Opportunity or the Department of Health, Education and Welfare. They provide full, comprehensive outpatient services and have arrangements with hospitals for inpatient care. Health Centers must have community boards which help make sure that the center will meet the people's health needs. For

---

[40]Ill. Stat. Ann. Ch. 111 ½, No. 86 (Smith-Hurd, as amended 1969); Calif. Health and Safety Code, No. 1407.5; Gen. Stat. of N. Car., Ch. 131. Art. 13A §131-126.7 (1947), and *Laws, Regulations and Procedures Applying to the Licensing of Hospitals in North Carolina*, Part III, p. 17 (1964). *Manlove v. Wilmington General Hospital*, 53 Del. 339, 169 A.2d 18 (1961), aff'd on other grounds, 54 Del. 15, 174 A.2d 135 (1961); *Santurf v. Sipes*, 447 S.W. 2d 558 (Mo. 1969).

[41]State tax exemption, see e.g., *Cleveland Osteopathic Hospital v. Zangerle*, 153 Ohio 222, 91 N.E. 2d 261 (1950); *Ruston Hospital v. Riser*, 191 So. 2d 665 (La. C.A. 1966). Federal tax exemption, see e.g., *Loraine Avenue Clinic*. 31 T.C. 141 (1958); *Sonora Community Hospital v. Commissioner*, 46 T.C. 519 (1966).

example, centers should be open in the evening if people need them then, and people who are well should be able to get health and social services.

If there is a health center in your neighborhood, it will normally provide services to everyone who is eligible for Medicaid or Medicare, plus to people who are poor or have low incomes but do not qualify for Medicaid. If you are eligible for Medicaid and you sign up for a government neighborhood health center, you must generally get all of your health services from that center. You cannot have the services of *both* the health center *and* a private doctor or clinic. An exception to this rule is made if the neighborhood health center does not provide services that are available to other recipients of Medicaid in your state in which case you will be able to continue to get these additional services outside the neighborhood health center.

No one eligible for Medicaid is required to use the neighborhood health center. If you sign up for a neighborhood health center and then don't like it, you can quit. This is what freedom of choice means under Medicaid.

C. PATIENTS' RIGHTS

What rights do patients have?

All patients, rich or poor, have a right to: (1) be treated with dignity and respect; (2) be examined and treated in privacy, behind closed doors or curtains and without extra people such as medical students or policemen being present; (3) have conversations with doctors and health workers and medical records kept confidential and not be released to outside agencies without written consent; (4) be told in detail what is wrong with them and how their condition can be treated; (5) refuse treatment altogether; (6) be told all the risks and possible side effects of treatment; (7) choose between different possible forms of treatment; (8) change their mind in the middle of treatment and refuse further treatment; (9) read and make changes in all printed forms they are asked to sign; (10) refuse treatment by a particular doctor and ask for a different doctor; and (11) refuse to be used for teaching purposes or for research purposes.

Rights of patients have been guaranteed by court decisions, statutes and regulations, medical and hospital ethics, and the Standards for Hospital Accreditation of the Joint Commission on Accreditation of Hospitals (JCAH). Although the JCAH program of hospital accreditation is voluntary, most major hospitals in the United States have JCAH accreditation, and must meet the JCAH standards. Since JCAH standards are the same in every state, the quotes are all from those standards.

YOUR RIGHT TO BE TREATED WITH DIGNITY AND WITHOUT DISCRIMINATION

The patient's most important right is to be treated with respect and dignity. This includes being addressed by your proper name, being treated with courtesy, and not being discriminated against because of race, economic status, or the nature of your condition. The JCAH standards say:

Equitable and humane treatment at all times and under all circumstances is such a right [of patients] . . . no person should be denied impartial access to treatment or accommodations which are available and medically indicated, on the basis of such consideration as race, color, creed, national origin or the nature of the source of payment for his care.

YOUR RIGHT NOT TO BE "DUMPED" ONTO ANOTHER HOSPITAL

A common type of discrimination against poor people in hosptial emergency rooms is to transfer people to a public hospital even though the first hospital could treat their condition. Hospital workers call this "dumping." JCAH standards say: "no patient should arbitrarily be transferred if the hospital where he was initially seen has means for adequate care of his problem." If a patient in serious condition is transferred, "The referring hospital must institute essential life-saving measures and provide emergency procedures that will minimize aggravation of the condition during transportation." The referring hospital must also get consent to the transfer from the hospital where the patient is being sent and must send with the patient a record of "the immediate medical problem."

YOUR RIGHT TO PRIVACY

You have a right to be examined and treated in a manner that maintains the privacy of your body. This means that a closed door or at least a drawn curtain should shield the patient from people walking by. Also people not involved in your care should not be present without your consent. The JCAH standards say:

Every individual who enters a hospital or other health facility for treatment retains certain rights to privacy, which should be protected by the hospital without respect to the patient's economic status or the source of payment for his care. Thus, representatives of agencies not connected with the hospital, and who are not directly or indirectly involved in the patient's care, should not be permitted access to the patient for the purpose of interviewing, interrogating or observing him, without his express consent given on each occasion when such access is sought. [Note, this includes medical students and policemen]

The design and furnishings of examination and treatment areas, in the emergency department and outpatient facilities as well as in other parts of the hospital, should be so planned as to facilitate the maintenance of the patient's privacy, and as far as possible, to shield him from the view of others.

YOUR RIGHT TO CONFIDENTIALITY

What the patient says, and what is said to him or about him, should be kept confidential. No one should talk about you within earshot of bystanders or call across the room for some item of personal information. The JCAH standards say: "Another important aspect of the patient's right to privacy relates to the preservation of the confidentiality of his disclosures. The setting in which the patient's history is taken, for example, should be such that he can communicate with the physician in confidence."

Confidentiality also protects your medical record. Except for certain requirements of law, such as reporting cases of venereal disease or gunshot wounds to public authorities, information from your medical record about your condition should not be released to outsiders, including public authorities, without written consent.

YOUR RIGHT TO KNOW WHAT IS HAPPENING

You have a right to know in detail what your condition is, what treatment the doctor recommends, and what the chances are that that treatment will work. The JCAH standards say: "The patient has the right to communicate with those responsible for his care, and to receive from them adequate information concerning the nature and extent of his medical problem, the planned course of treatment and the prognosis." In addition, you have a right to know the risks that a particular form of treatment, such as drugs or surgery, involves, what other possible forms of treatment there are, and how much time and money a particular form of treatment will involve. You must assert these rights to get them. Doctors often assume that patients are too ignorant to be told about their condition or don't want to know. If you want to know, ask questions.

If you are being treated by several doctors, you have a right to know which one has the over-all responsibility for your care. This is recognized by the JCAH: "In many large hospitals, the patient may be seen by several physicians during the course of his treatment. He has the right to know the identity of the physician who is primarily responsible for his care."

If a patient does not speak English, he has the right to an interpreter. The JCAH Preamble says: "In the matter of communication, ethnic and cultural considerations are highly significant, and should be taken into account by providing interpreters where language barriers are a continuing problem."

YOUR RIGHT TO REFUSE TREATMENT

You have a right to refuse treatment for yourself or your children. You may refuse any kind of treatment, or may refuse to be treated by a particular doctor and request a different doctor. You may refuse to be treated until you are given complete information about your condition or about the proposed treatment. You may consent to treatment and then change your mind at any time. The only time you may be treated without your consent is in a serious emergency where you may die or be seriously disabled unless you are treated immediately, and you are unconscious or otherwise physically unable to consent.

Hospitals often use printed forms that they ask patients to sign to indicate that they consent to treatment. You should never sign such a form without reading it carefully.

You may ask that it be explained and you may cross things out or make other changes before signing it.

The right to refuse treatment applies outside of hospitals too—in prisons, nursing homes, or in schools. Many schools try to deal with active children by giving them tranquilizers, even though the problem may be with the school and not with the child. Tranquilizers are often dangerous to a child and you should not let school officials force you to give your child any medication. Ask a doctor's advice and decide for yourself. Your child *cannot* be expelled from school for refusing to take pills.

You also have an absolute right to refuse to be used for teaching purposes or for research purposes. Although teaching and research are usually done on poor people, often without their consent, the fact of being poor or a ward patient does not reduce a patient's right to refuse to be a medical guinea pig. The JCAH says:

> In many teaching hospitals, and particularly in those which are closely affiliated with medical schools, all patients, regardless of their economic status, may be expected to participate to some extent in clinical training programs or in the gathering of data for research purposes. For all patients, regardless of the source of payment for their care, this should be a voluntary matter. The level of the patient's participation in such activities should in no way be related to the source of payment for his care.

All of these patients rights have also been recognized by the American Hospital Association (AHA). The AHA Patients Bill of Rights guarantees some rights not provided by the JCAH standards.

YOUR RIGHT TO KNOW HOW YOUR HOSPITAL OPERATES, HOW TO GET CONTINUOUS CARE AND HOW MUCH SERVICES COST

The AHA standards provide:

> The patient has the right to obtain information as to any relationship of his hospital to other health care and educational institutions insofar as his care is concerned. The patient has the right to obtain information as to the existence of any professional relationships among individuals, by name, who are treating him.

> The patient has the right to expect reasonable continuity of care. He has the right to know in advance what appointment times and physicians are available and where. The patient has the right to expect that the hospital will provide a mechanism whereby he is informed by his physician or a delegate of the physician of the patient's continuing health care requirements following discharge.

> The patient has the right to examine and receive an explanation of his bill regardless of source of payment.

> The patient has the right to know what hospital rules and regulations apply to his conduct as a patient.

You can obtain copies of the JCAH Standards by writing to them at 875 N. Michigan Avenue, Suite 2201, Chicago, Illinois 60611. You can get the AHA Patients Bill of Rights by writing them at 840 No. Lakeshore Drive, Chicago, Illinois 60611.

VI

Food Stamps

Who is eligible for food stamps?
There are two requirements for getting food stamps:
(1) you must have low income; and (2) you must have
few resources. Beginning January 1, 1974, food stamps
will not be available to anyone receiving aid to the Aged,
Blind, or Disabled.[1]

Whose income is low enough to qualify for food stamps?
All families in which everyone is on welfare are automatically financially eligible for food stamps.[2]

All other households must have a monthly income not
higher than:

MONTHLY INCOME

Household Size	48 States and D.C.	Alaska	Hawaii
1	$178	$214	$202
2	233	281	265
3	307	400	400
4	373	480	480
5	440	573	573
6	507	667	667
7	573	733	733

---

[1] 7 U.S.C. §2012(e).
[2] 7 C.F.R. §271.3(b).

8	640	813	813
each additional			
person	+53	+67	+67

The Income Work Sheet on page 113[3] shows you how to figure out your monthly income. All families, even those on welfare, should figure out their income on the work sheet. The less income you have per month, the less you have to pay for food stamps. The work sheet shows you what items can be deducted from income.

Example. If you pay more than ten dollars per month for medical expenses, all of those payments can be deducted from income. Or, if you spend more than 30 percent of your income on rent, that can be deducted from your income. The Income Work Sheet shows you all of these deductions.

Migrants, and other persons whose income is irregular may be eligible for food stamps all year round even though their income is too high in some months,[4] if their annual income is below the following amounts:

Number in Household	Annual Income
1	$2136
2	2796
3	3684
4	4476
5	5280
6	6084
7	6876
8	7680
each additional person	+636

If you are eligible under this annual standard and the head of the household is a migrant, farmer, or self-employed person you can either pay according to your average monthly income or according to the actual income

---

[3]FSP No. 1971—1.
[4]7 C.F.R. §271.3(c)(2)(ii).

you expect to receive each month. The rights of migrant workers are discussed fully in the last chapter of this book.

INCOME WORK SHEET[5]

I. *Do not count* as income any of the following:
   A. Income of any students under 18 years of age.
   B. In-kind benefits (such as free use of a house).
   C. Infrequent or irregular income (up to $30 every 3 months).
   D. Lump sum payments such as insurance settlements, sale of property—except when related to self-employment.
   E. Cash prizes; awards; inheritances; retroactive lump sum payments such as Social Security, Railroad Retirement Pension, income tax refunds. (You can exclude these as long as they are one-time payments.)
   F. All loans (except loans to be repaid after completion of the recipient's education).

II. *Add* all of the following *incomes* you have:
   A. Net salary
      1. Total monthly salary before *any* deductions ....
      2. *Subtract* 10% of your total monthly salary, up to $30. (Divide by 10) .... —
         subtotal ....
      3. Also *subtract* mandatory deductions (taxes, social security, union dues) .... —
      ....NET SALARY FOR FOOD STAMP PURPOSES .... #A

---

[5] 7 CFR 271.3(c)(1)(i).

B. Self-employment Income

    1. Gross income from self-employment ....

    2. *Subtract* the cost of producing that income (but do not include: (a) payments on income producing real estate; (b) payments on the cost of equipment, machinery, and other capital assets; (c) depreciation; (d) net loss sustained in any previous period) .... —

    ....SELF-EMPLOYMENT INCOME .... #B

C. Payments of a roomer .... #C

D. Payments of a boarder (no more than 2 roomers or boarders allowed):

    1. Full payment of a boarder ......

    2. Subtract $36 for each boarder .... —

    ....NET PAYMENT OF A BOARDER .... #D

E. Payment by a member of the household who only gives a part of his income to the household .... #E

F. Payments received as an annuity, pension, retirement or disability benefits, veteran's compensation, workmen's or unemployment compensation, old age compensation, survivor's compensation, or strike benefits .... #F

G. Public assistance or general assistance payments (welfare) .... #G

H. Payments from other government programs such as Work Incentive Program (WIN), Manpower Training, Agriculture Stabilization and Conservation Service Programs .... #H

I. Payment made on behalf of the household by a non-member of the household (other than for medical expenses) .... #I

J. Scholarships, educational grants (including loans for education to be paid back after the education is completed) .... #J

K. Rents, dividends, interest, royalties .... #K

L. Support and alimony payments .... #L

Add lines A-L............GRAND INCOME TOTAL ....

III. *Add* all of the following *deductions*

A. If your medical costs are more than $10.00 a month for your household, you get a deduction for the full amount of your medical expenses .... #A

B. Cost of child care necessary to permit household member to work .... #B

C. Extra expenses in case of disaster to the household, or a loss (such as theft) .... #C

D. Educational expenses (such as tuition and fees), even if cov-

ered by scholarships and fel-
lowships .... #D

E. Monthly court-ordered support
and/or alimony payments (that
you *pay out, not that you re-
ceive*)[6] .... #E

F. Add lines #A-#E to get........
subtotal deductions .... #F

G. If your rent plus utilities is
more than 30% of your income
after deductions, you get a dis-
count. Figure it this way:
1. GRAND INCOME
TOTAL (in
section II) .... #1

2. *Subtract* "subtotal
deductions"
(#F) .... #2—

3. This gives you
"income after
deductions" .... #3

4. Figure 30% of
your "income after
deductions" in
#3 [divide by 10
and multiply by
3] .... #4

5. Now put down
your rent plus
utilities .... #5

6. Bring down the
figure on line #4
and *subtract* it
from line #5 .... #6 —

––––––––––
[6] 7 C.F.R. §271.3(c)(1)(iii).

This result is
your shelter
deduction .... #G
_____

Add lines #F and #G and you
   get....TOTAL DEDUCTIONS ....
_____
═══════════════════════════════

IV. To find your INCOME USED TO DETERMINE
    FOOD STAMP ELIGIBILITY AND PUR-
    CHASE PRICES, do this subtraction:
    A. GRAND INCOME TOTAL ....
    _____
    B. *Subtract* TOTAL DEDUC-
       TIONS .... —
    _____
    C. FINAL INCOME (for eligi-
       bility and food stamp purchase
       prices) ....
    _____
    ═══════════════════════════════

NOTE: This is the figure that the Food Stamp Agency
       uses to see if your income makes you eligible
       for food stamps. Check this figure with the
       income eligibility standards p. 111 to see if
       you are eligible. Your income must be be-
       low the amount listed next to your house-
       hold size.

**What money and property can you keep while getting
food stamps?**

Families in which all members are receiving welfare
are automatically eligible for food stamps.[7] Other households can have no more than fifteen hundred dollars in
resources. The only exception to this is a household of
two or more people in which one person is over sixty
years old. In this case the amount of resources may be
up to three thousand dollars.[8]

---
[7] C.F.R. §271.3(b).
[8] 7 C.F.R. §271.3(c)(4).

When adding up the resources that you own, do not include: (1) your home or car; (2) property used in your work; (3) household goods and personal belongings; (4) life insurance; (5) resources or roomers or boarders or members of the household who give only part of their income to the household; or (6) Indian tribal lands.[9]

What is a "household" for getting food stamps?

A "household" for the purpose of receiving food stamps is a group of people who share the same living quarters (such as one apartment or house) *and* the same cooking facilities, are living as one economic unit, and buy food together.[10]

Do household members have to be related to each other?

No. In 1971 Congress passed a law saying that in order to get food stamps all the members of a household had to be related to each other.[11] The purpose of this law was to deny food stamps to hippy communes. In 1973 the Supreme Court said this law was unconstitutional.[12] Members of a household do not need to be related to each other.

Can you exclude some people from your food-stamp household?

Yes. If there are people living in your house or apartment who have large incomes, but who do not share their

---

[9] 7 C.F.R. §271.3(c)(4)(iii).
[10] 7 C.F.R. §§270.2 (jj) and 271.3 (a).
[11] 7 U.S.C. §2012(e).
[12] *Moreno v. U.S. Dept. of Agriculture*, 345 F.Supp. 310 (D.D.C. 1972), 409 U.S. 1036 (1973).

income with everyone in the house, these people might make you ineligible for food stamps.

If you want to exclude someone or a group of people from your food-stamp household, then those people should: (1) set up separate living quarters in the house; (2) cook and purchase food separately; and (3) live as a separate economic unit. The separate living quarters must have its own cooking facilities, but a hot plate is enough.

How do you apply for food stamps?

WELFARE HOUSEHOLDS

If you are getting welfare you should be immediately certified for food stamp program eligibility.[13] You should also bring with you any proof that would make you eligible for reduction of the cost of food stamps. For example, if your rent is more than 30 percent of your income after other deductions, you should take a rent receipt with you since that will reduce the amount you must pay for your stamps.

NONWELFARE HOUSEHOLDS

If some or all members of your household are not receiving welfare, you will have to fill out an application form and be interviewed in the welfare office, in your home, or by telephone.[14] When you first apply for food stamps, you will have to prove the amount of your income.

How soon can you find out if you will receive food stamps?

The welfare department must take your application and they cannot take longer than thirty days from the time you

---

[13] 7 U.S.C. 2019(c); 7 C.F.R. §271.4(a)(1)
[14] 7 C.F.R. §271.4(a)(2)(ii).

first ask for food stamps to decide whether or not you will get them.[15]

Do you have a right to continue receiving food stamps?
Every so often you must be recertified to receive food stamps.

You have a right to be certified for twelve months if your household is made up of unemployable persons and has a stable income, or your income is from self-employment, farming, or farm employment (migrant workers).

You have a right to be certified for six months if your income is likely to remain the same.

Other households will be certified for three months.[16] You should try to get certified for as long a period of time as possible to avoid the inconvenience of recertifying every three months.

In all cases, you have the right to be recertified before the end of your certification period. Near the end of your certification period, the welfare department must notify you that your certification period is ending.[17] To be recertified, you must have another interview. It can take place over the telephone.[18] You do not have to prove your income again if you still receive it from the same sources and the amount has not changed very much.[19]

What do you pay and receive under the food-stamp program?
The amount that you have to pay for these stamps depends on your income and family size. To find out the

---

[15] 7 U.S.C. §2019(e)(2). *Golden Gate Welfare Rights Organization v. Born,* 27 Cal. App. 3d. 1, 103 Cal. Rptr. 854 (1972). 2CCH Pov. L. Rpt. ¶15,799.
[16] 7 C.F.R. §271.4(a)(4)(iii)
[17] 7 C.F.R. §271.4(a)(3)
[18] 7 C.F.R. §271.4(a)(2)(ii)
[19] 7 C.F.R. §271.4(a)(2)(iii)

amount, take your final monthly income figure from the Income Work Sheet and then look at the food-stamp price chart on the next page until you find the category your income fits into. Next look across the chart to find your family size. Where these two columns meet you will find the amount you will have to pay (monthly) for your food stamps.

Is every food-stamp recipient required to register for work?

No. The following people never need to register to work: (1) people eighteen and under, or sixty-five and over; (2) mothers or other household members who must care for children under eighteen; (3) people who care for incapacitated members of their household; (4) students who are enrolled at least half-time in a school or training program; and (5) people working at least thirty hours a week. Everybody else must register for work when they first apply for food stamps, and when they are recertified.[20]

Can you refuse an unsuitable job offer?

To be suitable, a job must meet all of the following standards:

(1.) It must have wages which are at least as high as the highest of the following:

(a.) Federal minimum wage (if the job is covered by the Federal minimum wage);

(b.) State minimum wage, (if the job is covered by the State minimum wage); or

(c.) $1.30 an hour.[21]

This also applies for piece-rate work. The payment for average hourly yield for piece-rate work must meet these standards.[22]

(*This listing continued on p. 124*)

---

[20] 7 C.F.R. §271.3(e).
[21] 7 U.S.C. §2014(c). 7 C.F.R. §271.3(e)(3)(i).
[22] 7 C.F.R. §271.3(e)(3)(ii).

FOOD STAMP PRICE CHART

FOR A HOUSEHOLD OF

THE MONTHLY COUPON ALLOTMENT IS

AND THE MONTHLY PURCHASE REQUIREMENT IS

Income Monthly Net	1 Person $38	2 Persons $66	3 Persons $94	4 Persons $116	5 Persons $138	6 Persons $160	7 Persons $180	8 Persons $200
$ 0 to 19.99	$ 0	$ 0	$ 0	$ 0	$ 0	$ 0	$ 0	$ 0
20 to 29.99	1	1	0	0	0	0	0	0
30 to 39.99	4	4	4	4	5	5	5	5
40 to 49.99	6	7	7	7	8	8	8	8
50 to 59.99	8	10	10	10	11	11	12	12
60 to 69.99	10	12	13	13	14	14	15	16
70 to 79.99	12	15	16	16	17	17	18	19
80 to 89.99	14	18	19	19	20	21	21	22
90 to 99.99	16	21	21	22	23	24	25	26
100 to 109.99	18	23	24	25	26	27	28	29
110 to 119.99	21	26	27	28	29	31	32	33
120 to 129.99	23	29	30	31	33	34	35	36
130 to 139.99	25	32	33	34	36	37	38	39

Income		35	36	37	39	40	41	42
140 to 149.99	27	35	36	37	39	40	41	42
150 to 169.99	27	37	40	41	42	43	44	45
170 to 189.99	28	43	46	47	48	49	50	51
190 to 209.99		45	52	53	54	55	56	57
210 to 229.99		45	58	59	60	61	62	63
230 to 249.99		46	64	65	66	67	68	69
250 to 269.99			70	71	72	73	74	75
270 to 289.99			75	77	78	79	80	81
290 to 309.99			75	83	84	85	86	87
310 to 329.99			76	89	90	91	92	93
330 to 359.99				89	96	97	98	99
360 to 389.99				92	103	106	107	108
390 to 419.99					107	115	116	117
420 to 449.99					109	119	125	126
450 to 479.99					110	123	133	135
480 to 509.99						127	137	141
510 to 539.99						128	141	145
540 to 569.99							143	149
570 to 599.99							143	153
600 to 629.99							144	157
630 to 659.99								159
660 to 689.99								160

I. Household of more than 8 persons, use the following formula:

  A. *Value of the total allotment:* For each person in the household over 8 people, add $16 to the monthly coupon allotment for an 8-person household.

  B. *Purchase requirement:*

    1. Use the purchase requirement shown for the 8-person household for households with incomes of $599.99 or less per month.

    2. For households with monthly incomes of $600 or more, use the following: For each $30 worth of monthly income (or portion thereof) over $599.99, add $4 to the monthly purchase requirement shown for an 8-person household with an income of $599.99. For maximum monthly purchase requirements for households of more than 8 persons, add $12 for each person over eight to the maximum purchases requirement shown for an 8-person household.

(*Continued from page 121*)

  (2.) It must meet all the requirements for suitable work under the work incentive program. See page 53.[23]

  (3.) It must be a job that is in the person's major field of experience.[24]

  (4.) It must not require you to spend one fourth or more of your work time traveling to and from work. (*Example.* A person who is told to take a job that requires eight hours of work per day does not have to take the job if the travel time to and from the job is two hours a day, one hour each way.)[25]

All of these requirements must be met before a job is considered suitable. You do not have to accept any job that does not meet these standards.[26]

---

[23] 7 C.F.R. §271.3 (e).
[24] 7 C.F.R. §271.3(e)(5)(iii).
[25] 7 C.F.R. §271.3(e)(5)(iv).
[26] 7 C.F.R. §271.3(e)(3,4 and 5).

What happens when you refuse a job?

If the welfare department is threatening a cut off of your food stamps because you refused a job, immediately request a hearing. The welfare department cannot cut off food stamps if you request your hearing within fifteen days from the date you are told you must take the job. If you win the fair hearing you will not have to accept that job. If you lose, you must either accept the job, if it is still available, or stop receiving food stamps.[27]

Are welfare payments cut when a recipient gets food stamps?

No. Your welfare check, or any other assistance you get, cannot be cut, because you are receiving food stamps. If you start getting welfare while you are already getting food stamps, your food-stamp bonus cannot be counted as income when they decide how much you will get in your welfare check.[28]

When can you purchase food stamps?

Federal regulations say that you must be able to buy food stamps either once a month or twice a month, whichever is most convenient for your household. Each month you can choose whether to purchase stamps once or twice that month. The welfare department must also allow you to buy stamps more often than this if that is more convenient for many people in your county.[29]

---

[27] 7 C.F.R. §271.1(0)(5).
[28] 7 U.S.C. 2016(c); 7 C.F.R. §271.1(b and c).
[29] 7 C.F.R. §271.6(d)(4).

Do you have a right to buy only part of your food-stamp allotment?

Yes. Each month you can choose to buy either three fourths, one half, or one fourth of your food-stamp allotment for that month.[30] If you choose to buy only a percentage of your allotment, you pay only the same percentage of the price of your full allotment of stamps. Buying only a part of your full allotment of stamps does not take away your right to buy stamps either once or twice a month.

Are shopkeepers who serve food-stamp customers regulated?

Yes. Store owners must be certified by the Department of Agriculture before they can accept food stamps. When you use your food stamps, storekeepers cannot detach the coupons for you. They cannot make you use your food stamps for debts you owe them.[31] They cannot raise the price of food on the days people receive their food stamps. If a storekeeper is not treating people fairly, he can lose his authorization to serve food-stamp customers.[32] You can demand that the Department of Agriculture decertify stores unless they change their practices. Write:

> Director of the Food Stamp Program
> Food and Nutrition Service
> United States Department of Agriculture
> Washington, D.C. 20250

---

[30] 7 U.S.C. 2016(b); 7 C.F.R. §271.6(d)(3).
[31] 7 C.F.R. §272.2(d, e and g).
[32] 7 C.F.R. 272.1(e).

What rights to fair treatment do food-stamp recipients have?

You have a right to fair hearings in the food-stamp program just as in other welfare programs. See page 72 on hearing rights. This includes the right to a fair hearing any time the department takes any action that is harmful to a household that receives or applies for food stamps.[88] The department must notify you in writing fifteen days before any action is taken to cut off your food stamps and must give you an opportunity for a prior hearing.[84] You must be given fair opportunity to ask for a hearing—no special form is needed.[85] You must be given a chance to prepare, a fair "fair hearing," and a speedy decision.[86]

---

[88] 7 U.S.C. 2019(e)(6); 7 C.F.R. 271.1(o).
[84] 7 C.F.R. 271.1(h) and (n).
[85] 7 C.F.R. 271.1(o)(2).
[86] 7 C.F.R. 271.1(o)(2)(3) and (4).

VII

Free School Lunches

Must poor children get a free or reduced-cost lunch?

Yes. The promise of the National School Lunch Act is that "every child from a family whose income falls below the poverty line will receive a free or reduced price lunch."[1] Even though this is the law, all over the country many poor children attend schools in which there is no school lunch program. Many other children do not have the money to purchase a nutritious school lunch.

Must school boards provide free lunches to all poor children in the school district?

Yes. The School Lunch Act provides federal funds to school districts for free and below-cost school lunches. If a school district gets any money under this program, then the school board must provide school lunches for all of the children in the district.[2] They cannot just provide lunches for younger children. They cannot just provide lunches for schools in richer neighborhoods. They cannot use the fact that a school does not have kitchen facilities as an excuse to refuse to provide school lunches. If a

---

[1] Pres. Nixon, 116 Cong. Rec. 10541 (Daily ed. July 23, 1970).

[2] 42 U.S.C. §1758, 7 C.F.R. §245.3(a).

128

school does not have a kitchen, the school board must make other arrangements to make sure all children receive a nutritious lunch.

Which children have priority under the school lunch program?

The purpose of the school lunch program is to make sure that the poorest children will get free school lunches first. Within the United States, poor states get the most school lunch money.[3] Within the state, poor schools are given a preference.[4] Within a school, poor children must come first.[5]

The best way to find out whether a school is a poor people's school is to look at the school district's applications for money under Title I of the Elementary and Secondary Education Act. Schools that get Title I money are in neighborhoods with the most poor children.

Must poor children get a free or reduced-cost lunch?

Yes. Under the federal law, all children from families with income below the following levels must get a free or reduced-cost lunch.[6] A reduced-cost lunch cannot be more than twenty cents.[7]

The minimum levels and the maximum levels are listed below. The amounts represent annual income. They apply to all states except Alaska and Hawaii.

---

[3] 42 U.S.C. §1753. *Davis v. Robinson* 346 F.Supp. 847 (D.R.I. 1972).
[4] 42 U.S.C. §1757.
[5] 42 U.S.C. §1758.
[6] 7 C.F.R. 245.3.
[7] 42 U.S.C. §1758.

Family Size	MINIMUM Guidelines For Free Meals	MAXIMUM Guidelines For Free Meals	MAXIMUM Guidelines For Reduced-Price Meals
1	$2,190	$2,740	$3,280
2	2,880	3,600	4,320
3	3,570	4,460	5,360
4	4,250	5,310	6,380
5	4,880	6,100	7,320
6	5,510	6,890	8,260
7	6,080	7,600	9,120
8	6,650	8,310	9,980
9	7,170	8,960	10,750
10	7,680	9,600	11,520
Each Additional Family Member	+510	+640	+770

In some school districts free school lunches are available to families earning more income. Whatever eligibility standard is used, it must be the same for all children in the school district.

What rights are guaranteed under the school lunch program?

Every fall the school must send every parent a notice explaining children's rights to school lunches.[8] This notice must state:

(1.) eligibility standards for free and reduced-cost school lunches;

(2.) the name of the officials authorized to determine who is eligible for free or reduced-cost lunches;

(3.) a description of the free-lunch-application process;

(4.) a description of procedures used to keep the names

---

[8]7 C.F.R. §245.5(a).

of children who apply for free or reduced-cost lunches confidential; and

(5.) a description of appeals and hearing rights.

Eligibility for a school lunch is determined by the parents' declaration of income. If the information on the application form qualifies a child for free lunches, he must begin getting them right away.[9] If the school thinks that the child is not eligible for a free school lunch, the school can ask for a hearing,[10] but in the meantime their children must continue to get free or reduced-cost lunches.

Can children receiving free lunches be given special treatment?

No. In the past, many schools tried to make poor children work for their school lunches, or had special lines or lunchrooms or tokens for children receiving free or below-cost lunches. Of course, most children are upset and embarrassed at being singled out and labeled as "different."

All of these practices are now illegal.[11] Any physical segregation or other discrimination against children receiving free lunches is prohibited. The school can not use special tokens or tickets to identify poor children.

How can people get their rights under the school lunch program?

Many children and parents around the country have organized school lunch campaigns to get their rights. In other places lawsuits have been pressed to win school lunch rights. The people listed on page 14 can help you organize a campaign or lawsuit.

---

[9]42 U.S.C. §§1758.
[10]7 C.F.R. §245.6(b).
[11]42 U.S.C. §1758, 7 C.F.R. §245.8.

RIGHTS OF THE POOR IN VARIOUS STATES

Key to the chart. This chart was prepared in August 1971 and has not been kept up to date. Grant levels and eligibility rules change often. The chart will give you a rough idea of the differences among the states, and in different programs. However, you should not rely on it but should seek specific information from your local department of welfare.

GRANT LEVELS

The first six columns tell you the *amount of the monthly grant,* for a family of four, a couple or an individual. It assumes that there is no income except for welfare and that the family has no special needs which are recognized by the state. The amount listed is the amount that people should *actually receive.*

LIENS ON REAL PROPERTY

The little "x" in the grant-level boxes tells you whether the state requires that people receiving welfare must sign a lien on any real property that they own as a condition of receiving aid.

AID TO DEPENDENT CHILDREN WITH UNEMPLOYED PARENTS

If nothing is written in this column, it means that the state does not provide for ADCU.

PERMITTED RESOURCES

This tells you what resources you are allowed to keep when you apply for welfare.

RELATIVE RESPONSIBILITY

This tells you which relatives are responsible for each other. In every state husbands and wives are responsible for each other. In every state, parents are responsible for the support of their minor children. The numbers on the chart show additional legally responsible relatives.

(1.) Adult children are responsible for their parents.

(2.) Brothers and sisters are responsible for each other.

(3.) Grandparents are responsible for their grandchildren.

(4.) Adult grandchildren are responsible for their grandparents.

(5.) The state has no written legal definition of relative responsibility.

MEDICAID ELIGIBILITY

The roman numerals show which optional Medicaid coverage the state offers. The dollar figures are the eligibility levels for the medically needy in states which include them in Medicaid.

(I.) All children under twenty-one, who would be, except for age, eligible for ADC.

(II.) Medically needy people whose income and resources, after deducting medical expenses, are less than the specified amount. People who have enough for daily living, but not enough for medical expenses.

(III.) People who are in a medical facility, except in a facility for mental diseases or TB, who, if they left such a facility, would be eligible for public assistance.

(IV.) Close relatives caring for children under the age of twenty-one.

(V.) Persons over twenty-one who are receiving general assistance.

(VI.) All people who, except for income and resources, would be eligible under the state's general-assistance plan, and who earn less than the specified amount.

(VII.) The state has a "buy-in" agreement under which they pay the premiums for Part B, Medicare and the deductibles and co-insurance for Part A, for people who are both old and poor.

STATE	(eligible family of 4) AID TO DEPENDENT CHILDREN	(eligible couple) OLD AGE ASSISTANCE	(eligible individual) AID TO THE BLIND	(eligible individual) AID TO THE DISABLED
Alabama	$140/mo	$103/mo/ person	$75/mo	$79/mo
Alaska	$300/mo	$200/mo/ person	$200/mo	$200/mo
Arizona	$167/mo	$164/mo	$118/mo	$118/mo
Arkansas	$100/mo	$94/mo/ person	$94/mo	$94/mo
California	$215/mo	$195/mo/ person	$202/mo	$131/mo
Colorado	$153/mo plus $82 max- imum rent & utilities	$140/mo/ person	$58/mo plus shelter on an as paid basis	$58/mo plus shelter on an as paid basis

CHART 135

(eligible family of 4) GENERAL ASSISTANCE	(eligible family of 4) AID TO DEPENDENT CHILDREN (unemployed parent)	PERMITTED RESOURCES	RELATIVE RESPONSI-BILITY	MEDICAID ELIGIBILITY
$12.50/mo/ person 3 mo maximum	—	OAA, AD, ADC—homestead less than $2500 net; personal property less than $1000. AB—no limit on homestead personal property $1200	spouse, parent 1, 2	I, III, VII
$80/mo/ person	—	no limit on homestead; $500 cash or deposit; $1000 other real and personal property	spouse, parent 1, 2, 3, 4, 5, 6	III
$183/mo	—	homestead less than $8000; personal property less than $800 per person or $1200 per family	no legal provision 7	
$20/mo/ person 2 mo maximum	—	homestead less than $6500; other real or personal property less than $500/person or $1000/ family; life insurance policy less than $1000	7	I, III, VIII
no specific limit	$168/mo	no limit on homestead; other real & personal property $5000 net value or less. For ADC— real property $5000 net value & personal property less than $600	1, 2, 3	I, II, III, VII (267/mo/ couple; 392/ mo/family of 4)
varies county to county	$160/mo plus $82 maximum rent & utilities	no limit on homestead; real and personal property $1000 per person. ADC $1500 allowed for family of 4	7	I, III, VII

STATE	(eligible family of 4) AID TO DEPENDENT CHILDREN	(eligible couple) OLD AGE ASSISTANCE	(eligible individual) AID TO THE BLIND	(eligible individual) AID TO THE DISABLED
Connecticut	$189.60/mo plus shelter allowance up to maximum	$105.30/mo plus shelter allowance up to maximum	$56.85/mo plus shelter allowance up to maximum	$56.85/mo plus shelter allowance up to maximum
Delaware	$149/mo	$130/mo/ person $260/mo/ couple	$150/mo	$107/mo - in residential care facility
District of Columbia	$235.88	$159.59/mo	$112.50/mo	$112.50/mo
Florida	$133	$114	$114	$114
Georgia	$131	$87/person	$87	$87
Hawaii	$333	$175	$142	$142

CHART 137

(eligible family of 4) GENERAL ASSISTANCE	(eligible family of 4) AID TO DEPENDENT CHILDREN (unemployed parent)	PERMITTED RESOURCES	RELATIVE RESPONSI-BILITY	MEDICAID ELIGIBILITY
varies	—	no limit on homestead; personal property less than $600. ADC personal property limit $250	1, 2, 3	I, II, III, IV, VII ($2300/yr/person; $2900/yr/couple; $4400/yr/family of 4)
$118/mo/person	$187/mo	no limit on homestead; cash reserve less than $300; all other real or personal property considered a resource	1	I, VII
$238.50/mo	$238.50/mo	no limit on homestead; cash reserve to $300 per person or $500 per family	1, 2, 3	I, II, III, IV, VI ($2100/yr/person; $2800/yr/couple; $3560/yr/family of 4)
—	—	no limit on homestead; personal & real property may be held if income producing; cash reserve up to $600 per person, $1200 per family	7	I, III, VII
$124	$124	homestead up to specified amount; resources to $1000; other real & personal property to $800 per person. Life insurance to $1000	7	I, III, VII
$367	$367	homestead up to $25,000; other real & personal property to $225.00 per person	1, 2	I, II, III, IV, V, VI, VII ($1668/yr/person; $2784/yr/couple; $3840/yr/family of 4)

STATE	(eligible family of 4) AID TO DEPENDENT CHILDREN	(eligible couple) OLD AGE ASSISTANCE	(eligible individual) AID TO THE BLIND	(eligible individual) AID TO THE DISABLED
Idaho	$246	$202	$163	$163
Illinois	$292.98	$231.88	$184.58	$175.42
Indiana	$373.70	$247	$185.25	$185.25
Iowa	$243	$178	$144	$117
Kansas	$196 plus shelter allowance	$120 plus shelter allowance	$78 plus shelter allowance	$78 plus shelter allowance
Kentucky	$193	$160	$96	$96

CHART 139

(eligible family of 4) GENERAL ASSISTANCE	(eligible family of 4) AID TO DEPENDENT CHILDREN (unemployed parent)	PERMITTED RESOURCES	RELATIVE RESPONSI-BILITY	MEDICAID ELIGIBILITY
—	—	modest homestead allowed; negotiable assets up to $750	7	I, III, VII
$250.18	$286.44	homestead allowed; real property & personal property to $400/ individual or $600/couple; $300 per ADC family of 4	1, 2, 3, 4	I, II, III, VII ($2052/yr/ person; $2508/ couple; $3636/ family of 4)
—	—	homestead & income producing real property allowed. Reserves to $350 individual, $700, couple, $150 per ADC family	1, 2, 3	I, III, VII
varies county to county	—	homestead allowed; household goods less than $3000; car less than $2500; cash less than $450 per person, $800 per family, life insurance to $1000	1, 2, 3	I, III, VII
$140.80 plus 80% of shelter cost	—	moderate homestead allowed; other real property to $750; cash to $400 for 1 individual, $1000 for family; vehicle less than $750	1, 2, 3	I, II, IV, V, VII ($1600/ yr/person; $2200/yr/ couple; $3000/yr/ family of 4)
—	—	homestead allowed; other income producing property to $5000; other property to $1000; reserves in cash $500 individual, $1000 couple, $1500 family	7	I, II, III, VII ($1500/yr/ person; $1800/ yr/couple; $3000/yr/ family of 4)

STATE	(eligible family of 4) AID TO DEPENDENT CHILDREN	(eligible couple) OLD AGE ASSISTANCE	(eligible individual) AID TO THE BLIND	(eligible individual) AID TO THE DISABLED
Louisiana	$133	$188	$101	$66
Maine	$168	$115/person	$115	$115
Maryland	no set limit	no set limit	no set limit	no set limit
Massachusetts	$318.40	$246.60	no set limit	$166.70
Michigan	$305	$221	$171	$171

CHART 141

(eligible family of 4) GENERAL ASSISTANCE	(eligible family of 4) AID TO DEPENDENT CHILDREN (unemployed parent)	PERMITTED RESOURCES	RELATIVE RESPONSIBILITY	MEDICAID ELIGIBILITY
—	—	homestead to $5000; other property to $1750 individual, $2750 family; for APTD individual $400 maximum allowable resources	1, 2	I, III
no set limit	$168	homestead allowed; other property to $500 individual, $800 couple, $1000 for ADC family; life insurance to $1500 per individual	1, 2, 3, 5, 6	I, III, IV, VII
—	—	homestead allowed; other property to $300; life insurance to $1000 per individual, $500 per individual under 18	1, 2, 3	I, II, IV, V, VI, VII ($1800/yr/person; $2280/yr/couple; $3200/yr/family of 4)
$295.10	$336.60	homestead allowed; personal property to $2000 per individual in AB programs; $1000/ADC family; $1000/other individual. Life insurance to $1000	1, 2	I, II, III, IV, VII ($2160/yr/person; $2832/yr/couple; $4176/yr/family of 4)
varies county to county	$305	homestead allowed; other real property to $750 per individual or $1000 per family	1, 2, 3	I, II, III, IV, VII ($1900/yr/person; $2700/yr/couple; $3540/yr/family of 4)

STATE	(eligible family of 4) AID TO DEPENDENT CHILDREN	(eligible couple) OLD AGE ASSISTANCE	(eligible individual) AID TO THE BLIND	(eligible individual) AID TO THE DISABLED
Minnesota	$316	$218	$158	$158
Mississippi	$60	$65/person	$65	$65
Missouri	$130	$170	$90	$80
Montana	$206	$174	$123	$111
Nebraska	$192	$82 per person plus rent as paid	$82 plus rent as paid	$82 plus rent as paid

CHART   143

(eligible family of 4) GENERAL ASSISTANCE	(eligible family of 4) AID TO DEPENDENT CHILDREN (unemployed parent)	PERMITTED RESOURCES	RELATIVE RESPONSI-BILITY	MEDICAID ELIGIBILITY
$240	$320	real property to $7500 ($10,000 in CAA program); personal property to $300 per individual; life insurance to $500	1	I, II, VII ($1740/yr/person; $2424/yr/couple; $3456/yr/family of 4)
—	—	real property to $2500; personal property to $500 per individual, $1000 per family	7	I, III, VII
$280	$139	real & personal property to $10,500 in AB program; homestead allowed with other personal property to $2000	1, 2	I, III, V, VII
$206	$227.50 (incapacitated parent only)	real property less than $5000 when homestead; other real property to $1000; resources to $500; life insurance to $1000 per person	1, 2, 3	I, II, III, VII (less than 133% of most liberal income eligibility standard for categorical assistance)
varies county to county	$158	real property as home; other property to $3000, life insurance to $1000; other assets to $750, individual, $1500 couple, $1550 ADC family	7	I, II, VII $1600/yr/person; $2200/yr/couple; $3000/yr/family)

STATE	(eligible family of 4) AID TO DEPENDENT CHILDREN	(eligible couple) OLD AGE ASSISTANCE	(eligible individual) AID TO THE BLIND	(eligible individual) AID TO THE DISABLED
Nevada	$176	$266	$175	no program
New Hampshire	$124 plus shelter to overall maximum of $209	$158	$103	$103
New Jersey	$324	$222	$142	$142
New Mexico	$179	$155	$116	$116
New York	$208 plus rent & heating fuel	$134 plus rent & heating fuel	$84 plus rent & heating fuel	$84 plus rent & heating fuel
North Carolina	$189	$150	$115	$115

CHART   145

(eligible family of 4) GENERAL ASSISTANCE	(eligible family of 4) AID TO DEPENDENT CHILDREN (unemployed parent)	PERMITTED RESOURCES	RELATIVE RESPONSI-BILITY	MEDICAID ELIGIBILITY
varies county to county	——	real property as home to $7500; all other property to $750 individual, $1500 couple, $800 for ADC family of 4	7	I, III, VII
varies county to county	——	home and other real property to $1500 individual or $3000 family; personal property to $300 individual, $500 family; life insurance $2000 family	1, 2, 3	I, II, III, IV, VII ($2280/yr/person; $2868/yr/couple; $3744/yr/family of 4)
varies	$324 (incapacitated parent only)	homestead allowed; no specific limit on other real or personal property; life insurance to $1000 for person over 18	1, 2, 3, 5	I, III, VII
——	——	homestead allowed; personal property to $1200; life insurance to $550; cash to $100 individual or $150 family	1, 2	I, VII
$208 plus rent & heating fuel	$208 plus rent & heating fuel	homestead essential property allowed; life insurance to $500; trust fund for ADC child to $1000	1, 2	I, II, IV, V, VI, VII ($2500/yr/person; $3400/yr/couple; $5000/yr/family of 4)
——	——	homestead allowed; other real and personal property to $1000 individual, $1100 couple, $1200 family of 4; cash reserve for AB recipient of $600	7	I, II, III, IV, VI, VII ($1700/yr/person; $2200/yr/couple; $2800/yr/family of 4)

STATE	(eligible family of 4) AID TO DEPENDENT CHILDREN	(eligible couple) OLD AGE ASSISTANCE	(eligible individual) AID TO THE BLIND	(eligible individual) AID TO THE DISABLED
North Dakota	$300	$190	$125	$125
Ohio	$104 plus shelter to maximum	$64 plus shelter to maximum	$68 plus shelter to maximum	$58 plus shelter to maximum
Oklahoma	$188.70	$212	$130	$130
Oregon	$208.21	$176.80	$163.42	$122.21
Pennsylvania	varies county to county high $313 low $256	varies county to county high $218 low $164	$105	varies county to county high $146 low $102

CHART 147

(eligible family of 4) GENERAL ASSISTANCE	(eligible family of 4) AID TO DEPENDENT CHILDREN (unemployed parent)	PERMITTED RESOURCES	RELATIVE RESPONSI-BILITY	MEDICAID ELIGIBILITY
varies county to county	—	homestead allowed; income producing real property to $8000; other real property to $1000; cash reserve to $350	7	I, II, VII ($1800/yr/person; $2400/yr/couple; $3600/yr/family of 4)
$104 plus shelter to maximum	$104 plus shelter to maximum	homestead allowed ($12000 limit in CAA); income producing property allowed; other property to $300; life insurance $500 individual, $1000 family	1, 2, 3	I, III, VII
$20	$188.70	homestead to $8000; other property to $350 individual or $500 family	1, 2	I, II, IV, VII ($1400/yr/person; $2000/yr/couple; $3100/yr/family of 4)
$149.52	$231.84	homestead & other real & personal property allowed with no limit; liquid assets $500 individual or $1000 family	1, 2, 3	I, III, IV
varies county to county high $313 low $256	varies county to county high $313 low $256	no limit on homestead; life insurance to $500; for AB program; $5000 real & personal property, & income limit $2880 per year	1, 2, 3	I, II, III, IV, V, VII ($2000/yr/person; $2500/yr/couple; $4000/yr/family of 4)

STATE	(eligible family of 4) AID TO DEPENDENT CHILDREN	(eligible couple) OLD AGE ASSISTANCE	(eligible individual) AID TO THE BLIND	(eligible individual) AID TO THE DISABLED
Rhode Island	$255	$210.70	$162	$162
South Carolina	$105.46	$80	$95	$80
South Dakota	$270	$220	$180	$180
Tennessee	$129	$149	$97	$97
Texas	$104 plus shelter to maximum of $44	$159 plus shelter up to maximum of $33	$77 plus shelter to maximum of $33	$77 plus shelter to maximum of $33

CHART 149

(eligible family of 4) GENERAL ASSISTANCE	(eligible family of 4) AID TO DEPENDENT CHILDREN (unemployed parent)	PERMITTED RESOURCES	RELATIVE RESPONSIBILITY	MEDICAID ELIGIBILITY
$266.10	$266.10	homestead allowed; all other property considered a resource; cash up to $200 may be retained; life insurance to $1000	1, 2, 3, 5, 6	I, II, III, IV, VII ($2500/ yr/person; $3500/yr/ couple; $4300/yr/ family of 4)
$40	—	homestead allowed; property reserve of $750 individual, $1000 family; liquid assets of $750 individual or $1000 family	1, 2, 5	I, III, IV, V, VII
—	—	homestead allowed; other personal property to $1000 individual; $2000 couple, $1900 ADC family of 4; life insurance to $1000	1, 2, 3	I, III, VII
—	—	homestead and all real property to $9000; personal property to $500 individual, $1000 family	1, 2	I, III, VII
—	—	homestead allowed; other real & personal property to $1800 for individual, $3000 for family	1, 2	I, III, VII

STATE	(eligible family of 4) AID TO DEPENDENT CHILDREN	(eligible couple) OLD AGE ASSISTANCE	(eligible individual) AID TO THE BLIND	(eligible individual) AID TO THE DISABLED
Utah	$218	$138	$113	$103
Vermont	$223 plus shelter to maximum of $88	$159 plus shelter to maximum of $85	$100 plus shelter to maximum of $85	$100 plus shelter to maximum of $88
Virginia	no specific limit	no specific limit	no specific limit	no specific limit
Washington	$279	$212	$176	$176
West Virginia	$138	$97	$76	$76
Wisconsin	$151 plus shelter to area maximum of $130	$99 plus shelter to area maximum	$63 plus shelter to area maximum	$63 plus shelter to area maximum

CHART 151

(eligible family of 4) GENERAL ASSISTANCE	(eligible family of 4) AID TO DEPENDENT CHILDREN (unemployed parent)	PERMITTED RESOURCES	RELATIVE RESPONSI-BILITY	MEDICAID ELIGIBILITY
$218	$218	homestead allowed; other real & personal property to $600 individual, $1200 family; insurance to $500 individual, $1000 family; burial trust to $750 individual or $1500 family	1, 2	I, II, III, VII ($1500/yr/person; $2016/yr/couple; $3180/yr/family of 4)
emergency only; no on-going program	$223 plus shelter to maximum of $88	homestead allowed; real & personal property to $900 individual, $1800 family	1, 2	I, II, III, IV, VII ($2256/yr/person; $2964/yr/couple; $3828/yr/family of 4)
no specific limit	no specific limit	homestead allowed; other real & personal property to $1500; cash to $300; life insurance to $1500 face value	1, 2, 3	I, II, III, IV, VII ($1900/yr/person; $2500/yr/couple; $3300/yr/family of 4)
$279	$279	homestead allowed; cash assets to $400; life insurance to $1000	1, 2	I, II, V ($2232/yr/person; $2712/yr/couple; $3732/yr/family of 4)
—	$138'	homestead allowed; other real property and personal property to $1000	1, 2	I, III, VII
—	—	reasonable homestead allowed; insurance to $1000; liquid assets of $750, except ADC family which has limit of $500 liquid assets	1, 2, 3	I, II, III, IV, VII ($2600/yr/person; $3200/yr/couple; $3900/yr/family of 4)

STATE	(eligible family of 4) AID TO DEPENDENT CHILDREN	(eligible couple) OLD AGE ASSISTANCE	(eligible individual) AID TO THE BLIND	(eligible individual) AID TO THE DISABLED
Wyoming	$227	$178	$104	$104

CHART 153

(eligible family of 4) GENERAL ASSISTANCE	(eligible family of 4) AID TO DEPENDENT CHILDREN (unemployed parent)	PERMITTED RESOURCES	RELATIVE RESPONSI-BILITY	MEDICAID ELIGIBILITY
$200	——	homestead to $3000; other real & personal property to $500	1, 2	I, III

PART II

The Rights of
Migrant Workers

Given the reality of a migrant worker's existence, it is somewhat misleading to talk about his rights. So totally have migrants been omitted from American ameliorative social legislation, that what we would consider "rights" are assumed to be preconditions to civilized existence for most other people in our society.

The last piece of American social legislation that improved the position of agricultural laborers was the Emancipation Proclamation in 1863. The twentieth century New Deal legislation, which has provided the great mass of Americans with basic protection against economic catastrophe and exploitation, has simply bypassed the agricultural poor, leaving in its wake an invisible class of American serfs, trapped in a cycle of poverty and despair.

A. A Brief Introduction to the Mechanics of Migrant labor

Migrant agricultural labor is shaped by the rhythm of the harvest, which dictates that the bulk of the labor expended in agricultural production be telescoped into a comparatively brief part of the year. Agricultural en-

155

trepreneurs have therefore always sought to insure a ready source of agricultural labor at harvest time—and have always been plagued with the dilemma of what to do with the surplus labor during the rest of the year.

American farmers initially dealt with the need for a ready source of agricultural labor by the institution of slavery, which reduced agricultural laborers to the legal status of chattels.

After the abolition of slavery, agricultural entrepreneurs turned to the "patron" system, which dominated agricultural organization in the American West and the "tenant farmer" system which flourished in the South, both throwbacks to the feudal system which tied surplus labor to the lord's land on a year-round basis.

However, both the feudal form of organization and the use of slaves had one major economic drawback: while both were relatively efficient in guaranteeing a convenient source of agricultural labor at harvest time, each saddled the agricultural entrepreneur with economic responsibility for the surplus agricultural labor force during the remainder of the year. Accordingly, farmers evolved migrant agricultural labor as the dominant mode of agricultural organization in American life.

Migrancy is an ideal arrangement from the standpoint of the farmer, guaranteeing cheap agricultural labor on demand, while relieving him of any responsibility to the laborer during the nonharvest periods of the year. From the standpoint of the laborer, however, migrancy has been a disaster. Recruited from the most deprived strata of our rural poor, cut off from any stable community ties, lacking even rudimentary skills, constantly on the move from one alien surrounding to another, migrant agricultural laborers are condemned to an existence which can only be described as subfeudal.

More than 750,000 Americans are trapped in three national migrant streams.

The eastern stream flows from northern Florida, Louisiana, and Arkansas through Virginia and Maryland, into New York and New Jersey, with a comparative trickle continuing up to Maine. The migrants of the eastern stream are almost entirely black or Puerto Rican. As the harvest cycle passes from citrus fruits (northern Florida) to apples (Virginia) to potatoes, cherries, apples, strawberries, and truck farming (New Jersey and New York), the migrant travels from migrant camp to migrant camp to offer his labor to the waiting farmer. The central stream, made up of blacks, Chicanos, and whites, flows from Texas and Arizona to Michigan, Illinois, and Colorado. The western stream, which is predominantly Chicano, flows through California into Washington and Oregon.

Migrants generally travel in groups of between eight and thirty, called crews. Each group or crew is led by a crew chief (often called a labor contractor) who was himself once a migrant worker and who, by dint of resourcefulness and sheer physical strength, managed to gather a crew of his own. The crew leader negotiates with representatives of each farmer to furnish a given number of men at a certain time and place. The crew leader then recruits his crew (often with unrealistic promises and sometimes with naked threats of force), transports them to the harvest area, and establishes them in a migrant labor camp which is usually owned by the farmer but operated by the crew chief. Since a migrant ordinarily has no means of transportation other than the crew chief's bus, and since migrant labor camps are almost always built in remote places (presumably to spare the sensibilities of permanent residents), a migrant has no choice but to accept the "hospitality" of his crew chief.

Once established in a migrant camp, a worker is expected to eat his meals in the common mess hall. In most camps, the food concession is operated by the crew chief, who gains a substantial profit from it. In addition, each migrant is expected to pay a weekly rental to the crew chief for his dormitory cot. Each morning the crew chief transports his crew from the camp to the fields to await the farmer's instructions. Migrants are paid only for time actually worked, or on a piece-work basis. Thus, when weather, machinery breakdown, crop failure, or economic conditions make it impossible to work, they are simply not paid. This period, during which migrants are available for work but for which they are not paid, is called "down time." During down time, a migrant's fixed expenses for rent and food continue, creating a debt to his crew chief from which he rarely escapes. Often, a farmer will deliver a lump-sum wage payment to a crew chief, allowing the crew chief to deduct rent, food, and other outstanding debts before delivering the net-wage payments to the individual migrants. This device places the individual migrant entirely at the mercy of his crew chief. Should a migrant wish to challenge his crew chief's deductions, he knows, first, that the crew chief is a crew chief because he physically dominates his own crew and, second, that a migrant's only means of transportation back "home" is the crew chief's bus. In many locales, farmers unlawfully withhold a portion of a migrant's wages to insure that he will remain on the job until the harvest is completed. Often, this device takes the form of an artificially defined "bonus," which is really nothing more than the migrant's wages, payable at the conclusion of the harvest.

Migrants rarely, if ever, earn more than three thousand dollars in gross wages annually. An average migrant in the eastern stream is credited with about twenty hours of work per week after the subtraction of down time. He owes weekly fixed expenses of approximately twenty dollars for food and lodging to his crew chief and an average of five to ten dollars additional expenses for such "luxuries" as canned soda with meals, a pint of wine, and the right to watch the crew chief's television set. The weekly take-home pay of a fortunate eastern-stream migrant earning premium pay (two dollars per hour), in a good week, is about ten dollars. Migrants in the central and western streams fare no better.

THE EXCLUSION OF MIGRANTS FROM AMELIORATIVE SOCIAL LEGISLATION

The existence of such a system of wage peonage is made possible by the systematic exclusion of agricultural laborers from virtually all twentieth-century social legislation.

First, and most importantly, agricultural workers have been excluded from the protection of the National Labor Relations Act[1] *and from the "little Wagner Acts" enacted by the various states.* Only in Hawaii, Michigan, and the Commonwealth of Puerto Rico do agricultural workers possess collective bargaining rights comparable to those enjoyed by every other American worker. Moreover, in 1946, after some courts, sympathetic to the plight of agricultural workers, began to construe the agricultural exemption from the NLRA narrowly, the farm lobby succeeded in tacking a restrictive rider on the appropriations bill funding the National Labor Relations Board, prohibiting it from becoming involved in agricultural-labor disputes. This restrictive appropriations rider, which has had the effect of grafting a *de facto* amendment onto the National Labor Relations Act, has been approved annually by every Congress since 1946.

Since the National Labor Relations Act is designed to protect basic First Amendment associational rights, and since agricultural laborers are the only segment of American industry from whom such basic associational protections have been withheld, many persons have asserted that the agricultural exemption from the National Labor Relations Act denies agricultural workers the equal protection of the laws and, thus, is unconstitutional.

The Supreme Court has never ruled on a case directly involving the agricultural exclusion from the National

---

[1] 29 U.S.C. 152(3).

Labor Relations Act. However, at least one federal appeals court has ruled that the NLRA agricultural exclusion raises a substantial constitutional question.[2]

The major justification for excluding farmworkers from the protection of the National Labor Relations Act has been the assertion that agriculture is basically different from industrial production in that it is especially vulnerable to a strike involving perishable commodities. However, the experience of Hawaii and Puerto Rico indicates that agricultural collective bargaining can function constructively to protect workers without subjecting employers to costly strikes. Moreover, the experience of those seasonal industries dealing in perishable commodities, such as food processing, meat packing, freezing, and canning— all of which have operated profitably under the NLRA for years—indicates that collective bargaining functions admirably under precisely the conditions now prevailing in American agriculture.[3]

It should be noted, however, that coverage under the NLRA would not be an unmixed blessing for the nascent agricultural-union movement. Unquestionably their most potent weapon so far has been the boycott of those food chains carrying struck items. The outstanding example of this was the long and successful boycott by Cesar Chavez and the United Farmworkers Organization against food chains carrying grapes produced by struck farms. However, the Taft-Hartley Act, which applies only to labor unions as defined by the National Labor Relations Act, might well outlaw such tactics as an unfair labor practice. Whether the increased protection flowing to the migrant union movement from the provisions of the NLRA would

---

[2]*Local Union No. 300, Amalgamated Meat Cutters v. McCullough,* 428 F.2d 396 (5th Cir., 1970).

[3]The 1969 Report of the Senate Subcommittee on Migratory Labor (Rep't. No. 91-83, 91st Congress, First Session) provides an excellent discussion of the *pros* and *cons* of collective bargaining in agriculture. Copies of the report are available on request from the Committee on Labor and Public Welfare, United States Senate, Washington, D. C.

outweigh the dilution of its boycott power is, to many, an uncertain question.

It seems clear, however, that the current powerlessness of America's migrants flows directly from our refusal to permit them to organize for their own self-protection. Until such organizational protection is guaranteed, no substantial improvement in the lot of migrants is foreseeable.

Second, most agricultural workers are excluded from the minimum-wage–maximum-hour and the child-labor provisions of the Fair Labor Standards Act.[4] Even those few states, such as New York and California, which have provided for an agricultural minimum wage have discriminated against agricultural workers by providing for a minimum wage far below that set for all other workers. In addition, since minimum-wage laws are relatively ineffective in dealing with problems caused by piece-work compensation and down time, they have not substantially improved conditions, even when they exist.

Third, migrant agricultural workers, despite chronic unemployment and underemployment caused by down-time, are totally excluded from unemployment insurance.[5] Only Hawaii has provided for unemployment compensation to agricultural workers. In the past, the objection to extending unemployment compensation to agricultural workers has been the difficulty of keeping adequate records and the allegedly prohibitive cost involved. But the records that have been required by existing federal law[6] would be sufficient to administer an effective agricultural unemployment program. Nor is the prohibitive-cost objection any more persuasive. Opponents of agricultural unemployment compensation coverage argue that agriculture would be a "deficit industry," requiring the distribution of more money in benefits than it would raise by unemployment-insurance withholding taxes. However, even the most

---

[4] 29 U.S.C. §203(f).

[5] E.g. 26 U.S.C. §3306(c)(1)(k).

[6] In 1966, the FLSA was extended to apply to large farms, and agriculture was included under the SSA.

catastrophic projections of an agricultural deficit remain
substantially lower than the deficit currently existing in
the construction industry. Moreover, all estimates agree
that the deficit position of agriculture would be less
onerous than the fishing, canning, and construction industries—all of which currently enjoy unemployment-
insurance protection.

Despite the strong case for agricultural-unemployment
insurance, a divided federal court has recently refused
to declare the agricultural exclusion unconstitutional.[7]
However, additional litigation in this area is a virtual
certainty.

Since migrancy is a national problem, since the flow
of migrants is interstate, and since the federal government
is so intimately involved in the recruitment and placement
of migrants, many persons have urged a national program
of unemployment compensation for agricultural workers,
or, at the least, an interstate compact of migrant-using
states to provide unemployment insurance coverage comparable to that enjoyed by all other workers in America.

*Fourth, migrant agricultural workers are excluded from
compulsory workman's compensation and disability coverage in most states.* Despite the fact that agriculture is now
the third most dangerous occupation in the United States—
and getting more dangerous all the time with increased
mechanization and use of harmful chemicals—farm workers are denied the basic protection against occupational
accidents guaranteed to all other American workers. Only
California, Connecticut, Hawaii, Massachusetts, Ohio,
Puerto Rico, and Vermont provide full compulsory workman's compensation for migrants, while Alaska, Arizona,
New Hampshire, New Jersey, New York, Oregon, South
Dakota, Wisconsin, and Wyoming provide coverage on a
limited basis. Alabama and the District of Columbia pro-
hibit even voluntary coverage.

---

[7]*Romero v. Hodgson*, 319 F.Supp. 1201 (N.D. Calif., 1970),
aff'd §403 U.S. 901 (1971).

The federal government has recently enacted a workmen's-compensation plan for longshoremen. A similar plan for migrant agricultural labor is a critical necessity, since the plight of an injured migrant is exacerbated by the fact that the fixed expenses for rent and food owed to his crew chief continue to mount during the period of a migrant's disability.

Fifth, migrant agricultural workers are discriminated against in the administration of the Social Security Act. The Social Security Act is the only major piece of social legislation which does not explicitly exclude farmworkers. However, because of a discriminatory qualification requirement,[8] many agricultural workers are denied coverage, even though Social Security deductions from their salaries may have, in fact, been made. The Social Security Act requires that a migrant earn one hundred fifty dollars in cash from a single employer during a given year in order to qualify for Social Security coverage. Since, by definition, migrants rapidly change employers, many fail to meet that requirement and are thus deprived of coverage. Moreover, a farmer who may have erroneously withheld Social Security deductions from a migrant's wages often cannot trace the migrant (even if he tries) in order to refund the money.

Since migrant agricultural workers are excluded from the collective-bargaining protection of the National Labor Relations Act, the minimum-wage–maximum-hours protection of the Fair Labor Standards Act, the child-labor provisions of the Fair Labor Standards Act, the coverage of federal and state unemployment-compensation laws, the coverage of workmen's-compensation laws, and enjoy only restricted coverage under the Social Security Act, their current plight should come as no surprise. Yet, even within the framework of such systematic neglect of farmworkers, it is possible to ameliorate the harshness of their existence by requiring strict adherence to those few elemental rights

---

[8] 42 U.S.C. §409(h)(2)

which we have conferred upon them. The remainder of this chapter is devoted to a discussion of the rights migrants currently possess and practical suggestions for their enforcement.

B. The Current State of "Migrants' Rights"

Do persons interested in aiding migrants have a right to visit them on a migrant labor camp, even though the camp is the "private property" of a farmer or crew chief?

For years, farmers and crew chiefs were able to insulate migrants from the outside world by refusing to permit "outsiders" to "trespass" on a migrant labor camp. However, it is now clear that migrants possess a constitutional right to access to the outside world and that interested persons may visit them without regard to no-trespassing edicts. Two recent court decisions establish an unquestioned right of access to privately owned migrant camps for the purpose of visiting migrants and informing them of their legal rights.[9] The recent decisions merely restate, in the context of migrant camps, the Supreme Court's long-standing refusal to permit employers to bar outsiders from privately owned "company towns." *Marsh v. Alabama,* 326 U.S. 501 (1946).

Do migrants enjoy any minimum-wage protection?

Prior to 1966, migrants were completely excluded from minimum-wage protection. In 1966, the Fair Labor Standards Act was amended to grant minimum-wage protection of $1.30 per hour to those migrants employed on large farms. A large farm is defined as one which employed five hundred man-days of agricultural labor in any quarter

---

[9] *New Jersey v. Shack,* 58 N.J. 297, 277 A.2d 369 (1971); *Folqueras v. Hassle,* Civ. No. 242 (W.D. Mich., Sept. 7, 1971).

of the preceding year. Thus, if a farmer employs five migrants over a ten-week harvest period, he probably falls under the coverage of the federal minimum-wage law. Such a farmer must pay at least $1.30 per hour and must keep adequate financial records to document his compliance. If you suspect a violation of the federal minimum wage, report it to the local office of the United States Department of Labor. Any migrant who has been underpaid in violation of the minimum wage is entitled to sue individually for back wages and for punitive damages in federal district court.

In addition to federal minimum-wage protection (which is confined to migrants working on large farms), several migrant-using states have recently enacted a state agricultural minimum wage (the highest is New York's $1.50 per hour) which applies to all migrants.[10] Unfortunately, the states have not enforced the new minimum-wage legislation.

Moreover, two unresolved issues make the current minimum-wage protection of limited value. First, it is unclear whether down time is to be included in computing the actual hourly wages received by migrants. Since a migrant is available for work and has placed himself at the farmer's disposal, down time should be included in computing the hourly wage. Most state statutes, however, attempt to exclude down time in computing the actual hourly wage received by a migrant. Second, it is unclear whether migrants compensated on a piece-work, rather than a hourly, basis are protected. However, it would be absurd to permit a farmer to avoid minimum-wage coverage merely by electing a piece-work method of compensation. Thus, all wages should be converted to an hourly basis (including down time) in determining whether the minimum wage is being paid.

In addition, those migrants who have been recruited

---

[10]California; Hawaii; Massachusetts; Michigan; New Jersey; New Mexico; New York; Oregon; Puerto Rico; & Wisconsin have State minimum wage protection for migrants.

through the Interstate Employee Recruiting Service[11] enjoy two significant protections.

First, 20 C.F.R. §602.10(a)(h) guarantees each worker employment for at least 75 percent of the period specified on the work order. Thus, some protection is afforded against the chronic underemployment problem caused by down time.

Secondly, 20 C.F.R. §602.10(b) establishes a schedule of minimum-wage rates for each state which expressly supersede piece-work rates.

Since such provisions may prove expensive to the farmers involved, they will undoubtedly deny that they recruited through the Interstate Employee Recruiting Service. However, even if the farmers' current crew was recruited without the direct aid of the service, if one traces his contacts it is probable that his contacts were established years ago with the aid of the service. To the extent that the farmer continues to use such contacts to recruit, he should continue to be bound by the federal regulations.

Do migrants have any redress against misrepresentation concerning the terms and conditions of their employment?

Many migrants are induced to join a particular crew on the basis of representations concerning wages and living conditions. When those representations turn out to be false, migrants have several effective legal remedies.

First, many migrants are recruited through the machinery of the United States Interstate Employment Security Service and the Wagner-Peyser Act of 1933.[12] In

---

[11]The Interstate Employee Recruiting Service, a division of the United States Training and Employment Service of the Department of Labor, was created by the Wagner-Peyser Act of 1933 (29 U.S.C. 49-49L). It is designed to facilitate the interstate flow of labor and has played a major role in the growth and operation of the migrant labor system. Its activities are discussed in detail at 20 C.F.R. §§602 and 604.

[12]29 U.S.C. §49-49L.

the ordinary case, a migrant-using state will forward a "work order" to the United States Interstate Employment Recruiting Service, which, in turn, forwards it to a migrant-supplying state. The work order must describe the proposed terms and conditions of employment and any farmer availing himself of the facilities of the Interstate Employment Recruiting Service impliedly warrants that he will comply with the terms and conditions described in the work order. Any deviation from the described terms and conditions of employment gives rise to a federal suit for damages under the Wagner-Peyser Act.

Often, however, the misrepresentations involved were made not by the farmer but by the crew chief. The giving of false or misleading information by a crew chief may give rise to a federal suit for damages under the Farm Labor Contractor Registration Act.[18] The measure of damages in both situations would require the defendant to live up to his original representation.

Do migrants have any protection against improper deductions from their pay?

Any farmer who falls under the coverage of the Fair Labor Standards Act must keep detailed payroll records reflecting payments to his workers. Each migrant is entitled to a written statement of wages, with a written description and explanation of each deduction. However, many farmers turn their payrolls over to the crew chief for distribution to the individual migrants. It is totally improper (but very common) for the crew chief to make additional deductions for food, rent, and other debts prior to distributing the net wages to his men. Since it is the primary responsibility of the farmer to pay his employees, he remains liable to a migrant who has had money wrongfully withheld by a third person, including the crew chief.

As a practical matter, the most effective method of

guarding against improper deductions is to insist that the
farmer pay his employees directly instead of permitting
the crew chief to distribute the payroll. Preferably, payment should be made by payroll check (since the check
creates a built-in record of earnings). However, if payment is made by check, provision must be made to permit migrants to cash their checks nearby, or else the crew
chief will provide a check-cashing service and make his
"deductions" on the spot.

Deductions for Social Security payments are proper
only if the migrant has a Social Security number and
has earned at least one hundred fifty dollars in cash from
a single employer in the past year.[14] Again, as a practical
matter, all Social Security deductions should be inde-
pendently reported to the local office of the Internal
Revenue Service to insure that migrants get the benefit of
the coverage.

The statement of wages should be compared with the
representations contained in the work order or made by
the crew chief to determine whether the Wagner-Peyser
Act or the Farm Labor Contractor Registration Act has
been violated.

**Are there limits on the amounts which a crew chief
can charge for food and lodging in a migrant camp?**

The operation of migrant labor camps is closely regulated by statute in virtually every migrant-using state. In
New York, for example, a migrant camp operator may
not charge more than $16.50 for twenty-one meals or
more than $4.55 per week per bed. If the amounts charged
in your area exceed these figures (even outside New York)
a complaint should be filed with the state labor department.
A common device for circumventing statutory maximums
involves serving only water with meals. Migrants wishing

---

[14]For the purposes of the $150 computation only a crew-
chief may be viewed as a migrant's employer.

a beverage other than water are required to pay an additional fee. Such a practice clearly violates the intent of the statutory maximum and is illegal.

What can be done about a crew chief who abuses his position to the detriment of his men?

The Farm Labor Contractor Registration Act requires crew chiefs operating in interstate commerce to be licensed by the federal government. In addition, several migrant-using states require crew chiefs to obtain state licenses. Unfortunately, thus far, the licensing requirements have been largely ignored as a device in policing crew chiefs.[15] If you suspect a crew chief of wrongdoing, you should file a complaint with the licensing authority. More importantly, a crew chief who abuses his trust is vulnerable to court action aimed at voiding his license and putting him out of business.

Does a migrant have a right to decent housing while in a migrant labor camp?

Any farmer who uses the Interstate Employee Recruiting System impliedly warrants that the housing conditions in his camp will meet the minimum standards set forth at 20 C.F.R. §§620.1-620.17, which guarantee the following minimum conditions:

(1.) Housing sites providing adequate drainage and sewage disposal.

(2.) An adequate water supply (running water in a migrants' quarters is not required by the federal regulations, but is required by many state health codes).

(3.) Adequate provisions for sewage or septic-tank dis-

---

[15]At last count, only five employees have been assigned by the United States Department of Labor to administer the crew-chief licensing laws.

posal of human waste (indoor plumbing is not required).

(4.) Structurally sound housing units with flooring.

(5.) Adequate space requirements of at least sixty square feet of floor space per occupant.

(6.) Windows in all rooms, with adequate screening.

(7.) Heating equipment capable of maintaining a temperature of 68 degrees with adequate precaution against fire.

(8.) All housing sites must be provided with electricity and safe wiring.

(9.) Toilets for each sex in a ratio of not less than one unit for each fifteen occupants. Toilet facilities must be located within two hundred feet of each living unit.

(10.) Bathing and hand-washing facilities must be provided, with hot and cold running water, within two hundred feet of each living unit. A minimum of one showerhead for each fifteen occupants must be provided.

(11.) Laundry facilities must be provided in the ratio of one laundry tub to each twenty-five occupants or one washing machine to each fifty occupants.

(12.) Adequate containers for garbage must be provided adjacent to each unit. Refuse must be collected at least twice weekly.

(13.) Individual cots must be provided. If double-decked beds are used, thirty-eight inches of clearance must exist between the top bunk and the ceiling.

(14.) Adequate fire-escape exits must be provided.

(15.) No pesticides or chemicals may be stored in the housing area.

In addition, every migrant-using state has enacted legislation establishing minimum housing and sanitary conditions in migrant labor camps. These state codes are rarely enforced. The federal minimum standards provide a starting point for private inspection in the event state officials lack either the manpower or the will to enforce their own codes. To the extent conditions in a migrant labor camp fall below the standards set forth in the regulations, detailed complaints should be made to local health officials and the United States Employment Service.

Is there any way for a migrant to enforce his right to adequate housing?

Local health officials have been notoriously lax in enforcing even the minimal housing guarantees contained in the state health codes. If you believe that conditions in a migrant labor camp violate health standards, make a complaint in writing to the local health department and demand an immediate investigation with a written report of its findings. In demanding an investigation, it has proved helpful to submit photographs of the camp in question.

If local officials fail to do their job, federal courts have ruled that any migrant recruited with the help of the Interstate Employee Recruiting System may sue to enforce a farmer's implied 'promise to conform to the minimum housing standards set forth at 20 C.F.R. §§602; 604; and 620.1-620.17. Any violation of the federal standards should be immediately reported to the United States Employment Service to insure that the farmer involved will be barred from the use of federal recruiting facilities until the violations are remedied. Moreover, to the extent that the federal housing violations are attributable to laxity on the part of local officials in enforcing their own laws, federal courts have ruled that the local officials (such as the county health officer and state employment officials) may be sued in federal court to force them to do their jobs. The most important case in this area is *Gomez v. Florida State Employment Service,* 417 F. 2d 569 (5th Cir., 1969).

In addition to suing local health officials in federal court, they can be sued in state court to compel them to carry out their responsibilities. In connection with either the federal or state suit, you should demand copies of all inspection reports and an explanation of what follow-up action, if any, was taken.

Finally, every migrant-using state requires that the owner or operator of a migrant labor camp secure a license or permit to operate his camp. As a precondition to receiving such a license, a migrant-labor-camp operator must comply with health and sanitation codes. Thus, any suspected health violations should be reported to the licensing authorities with a formal notice of opposition to the renewal of the license involved. Finally, habitual offenders may be subjected to court action designed to void their licenses permanently.

May a farmer seek to avoid his responsibilities to migrants by claiming that they are really the employees of the crew chief?

One of the oldest dodges utilized by farmers in avoiding their responsibilities (both legal and moral) to migrant agricultural laborers has been to regard migrants as employees of their crew chiefs, thus severing any direct legal relationship between migrants and farmers. However, under the traditional master-servant law and under federal statutory law, it is clear that a direct-employment relationship exists between a farmer and the migrant laborers who harvest his crop. Thus, any attempt by a farmer to shift ultimate legal responsibility for the terms and conditions of a migrant's employment to a crew chief is incorrect. As the employer, it is a farmer's responsibility to control his crew chief, and to the extent he is unable—or unwilling—to do so, he bears ultimate legal responsibility for the acts and omissions of his foremen.

Can migrants be denied food stamps, health care and welfare payments on the ground that they are not residents of the state involved?

The nature of migrancy dictates that migrants must spend the major portion of the year in states other than their domicile. Several states have attempted to abdicate their responsibilities toward migrants on the ground that they are "transients" as opposed to "residents." However, it is now clear that no state can deny benefits to a migrant on the ground that he is not a resident.

In *Shapiro v. Thompson*, 394 U.S. 618 (1969), the Supreme Court ruled that residence requirements for welfare payments were unconstitutional. Following the *Shapiro* case, migrants have been ruled eligible for ADC payments despite their lack of intent to remain permanently. Moreover, migrants have been ruled eligible to receive food stamps despite the fact that they own a home in another state to which they plan to return.

Do migrants have the right to vote?

Migrants, of course, are entitled to register and to vote at their permanent residences. They are entitled to vote by absentee ballot if they will be out of state on election day. Moreover, under the Voting Rights Act of 1970, durational residence requirements of more than thirty days in Presidential elections are illegal. Thus, it should be possible for those migrants who have worked for thirty days prior to a Presidential election in a given state to vote for President in that state.

Do migrants have any protection against actions taken in retaliation for claiming their rights?

Since fear of employer or crew-chief retaliation is a constant and understandable deterrent to the assertion of a migrant's rights, it is always advisable to proceed anonymously, if possible. There are abundant precedents in the litigation surrounding birth control and abortion for using "John Doe" pseudonyms and there is no reason why the identities of actual complainants need be made public.

To the extent that crew chiefs and migrant-camp operators are licensed, they become instruments of government. Therefore, any retaliatory action should create a cause of action under Title 42 U.S.C. §1983—the Civil Rights Act. Moreover, Title 42 U.S.C. §1985 has now been construed by the Supreme Court to outlaw private conspiracies to deny persons their civil rights.

Despite the fact that agricultural workers are excluded from the protection of the National Labor Relations Act, California and Washington have recently recognized an independent right to organize and have ruled that retaliatory action aimed at impeding organization is illegal. It is highly probable that the remaining migrant-using states will follow suit.

Finally, attempts at retaliatory eviction have been branded illegal in several federal courts. Moreover, in most states, a landlord cannot evict tenants without complying with formal court procedures. Therefore, any attempt to evict migrants who are demanding their rights cannot proceed in the absence of a court order.

Do migrants have any rights under the National Labor Relations Act?

Persons engaged in agricultural labor have been exempted from the protection of the National Labor Relations Act. However, the term "agricultural labor" has received a narrow construction in the courts and many tasks, which to the layman would appear to be "agricultural," have been found to come within the Act's protection. Thus, migrants employed in grading and processing harvested items grown by a third person are probably within the protection of the National Labor Relations Act. As a rule, however, the NLRB will not deal with complaints arising on small farms. Thus, unless the farm in question does at least fifty thousand dollars' worth of business in interstate commerce, the NLRB will probably refuse jurisdiction. If a migrant is employed as a grader or processor on a large farm, the odds are he qualifies for NLRA protection. If any retaliatory action is taken or threatened against such an employee, an unfair-labor-practice claim should be filed with the local office of the National Labor Relations Board.

Have any special programs been instituted to aid migrant workers?

Federal programs to aid migrants do exist, although they are woefully underfunded. The Office of Economic Opportunity has funded a number of legal offices designed to provide lawyers for the rural poor. Whatever small legal gains migrants have made in the last five years are attributable, in large part, to the efforts of OEO lawyers. If an OEO legal services office exists in your community, it could play a major role in policing migrant labor camps and expanding migrants' rights.

In addition to the legal services offices, the OEO has established a number of projects designed to provide nonlegal assistance to migrants. These projects have sought to find permanent employment for migrants; conducted educational programs; provided transportation and even established food cooperatives. Local efforts to ameliorate the plight of migrants can be effectively channeled through such a project.

CONCLUSION

The fact that our law has progressed to the point where we guarantee migrants the "right" not to be forced to defecate in an open field hardly qualifies as a monument to America's social conscience. Moreover, even the minimal "rights" which have been bestowed upon migrants are honored far more in the breach, than in reality. Indeed, since migrants, as perhaps the most powerless segment in American society, are not in a favored position to claim even the pittance to which they are legally entitled, no substantial improvement in the conditions under which they live are foreseeable unless and until we include agricultural laborers within the mainstream of our social-welfare legislation. Only after agricultural workers are recognized as equals before the law can we hope for them to enjoy true equality in fact.

SYLVIA LAW is an assistant professor at the New York University School of Law, teaching women's rights, health law, and torfs. In 1966 she began working with New York City welfare recipients as a law clerk at Mobilization for Youth, and did welfare test case litigation at the Columbia Center on Social Welfare Policy and Law. She was the first staff director on the University of Pennsylvania's Health Law Project, an O.E.O.-funded program to establish individual rights to quality health services.

BURT NEUBORNE, a graduate of Harvard Law School, is assistant legal director of the American Civil Liberties Union. He is co-author of the 1973 Supplement to *Political and Civil Rights in the United States,* and he teaches a course in constitutional litigation at the New York University School of Law.